Medicine
for the
Mind

Healing Words to help you Soar

SECOND EDITION

Christopher P. Neck, Ph.D.

Virginia Polytechnic Institute and State University

Mc Graw Hill **Custom Publishing**

Boston   Burr Ridge, IL   Dubuque, IA   New York   San Francisco   St. Louis
Bangkok   Bogotá   Caracas   Lisbon   London   Madrid
Mexico City   Milan   New Delhi   Seoul   Singapore   Sydney   Taipei   Toronto

The **McGraw·Hill** Companies

Medicine for the Mind
Healing Words to help you Soar

1 2 3 4 5 6 7 8 9 0 MER MER 0 9 8 7 6

ISBN-13: 978-0-07-354329-1
ISBN-10: 0-07-354329-2

Editor: Ann Hayes
Production Editor: Kathy Phelan
Cover Design: Fairfax Hutter
Printer/Binder: Mercury Print Productions

Medicine for the Mind

Healing Words to Help You Soar

Christopher P. Neck, Ph.D.

Dedication

This book is dedicated to my wife Jennifer.   Jumper, while I certainly have changed over the years, there is one thing that will never change…..…my intense love for you.

Medicine for the Mind (2nd Edition) is additionally dedicated to my children Bryton, and GiGe.   You both have truly made my life, magical.

It is also dedicated to all of my students who have believed in me, inspired me, and encouraged me to try new ways of teaching.

Contents

Acknowledgment

An ancient proverb reads: "When the pupil is ready, the teacher will come." With this saying in mind, I have been quite fortunate to have various "teachers" come into my life at critical moments - moments when I was questioning who I was, the direction of my life, and my abilities; moments when I truly needed some "medicine for the mind" to restore my positive spirit. These individuals indirectly have contributed significantly to this book through their wisdom and advice to me over the years. In particular, I am indebted to Brent Neck, Heidi Neck, Mary Helen Neck, Susan and Tommy Neck, Ione Wilbert, Charles Manz, Joseph P. Patin, Banks Adams III, Glenn Sumners, Art Bedeian, Hank Sims, David Colvin, Dick Heinrich, Sanjay Goel, Peter Gariboldi Damian Luckett, and Stuart Mease for helping me to believe in myself.

I gratefully acknowledge the special inspiration I have received from the work, ideas, and thoughtful encouragement of Mike Goldsby, Jeff Houghton, Chuck Koerber, Krishna Kumar, Greg Moorhead, Rhonda Reger, Peter Hom, Dick Montanari, Harry Domicone, Dale Brown, Tom Keller, Bob D'Intino, Wanda Smith, Robert Ashcraft, Jeannette Eckert, Matt Cohn, John Milliman, Robin Hanson, Jeff Godwin, Bryan Dennis, and Arnie Kleiner.

In addition, I want to express my appreciation to the people at McGraw-Hill for their assistance in converting my ideas into a book. I want to extend a special thanks to J.D. Ice and Lorna Brown without whose encouragement and suggestions regarding the publication process this book might never have become a reality. Also, I want to express my gratitude to Ann Hayes, Christine Bowie, and Fairfax Hutter for helping to make the 2nd edition of this book a reality. I'd also like to thank Karen Poe in the Management Department at Virginia Tech for her invaluable editing assistance on this second edition.

Next, I'd like to recognize my son, Bryton, and my daughter, Gige, for all the joy they bring to my life. Thank you both for helping me to distinguish between what is truly important in my life and what is really "small stuff".

Finally, my best friend and partner-in-life, Jennifer, deserves my heart and my sincere thanks. Jen, in her own way, contributed to the ideas in this book through her patient listening to yet another newly written poem or story, her diplomatic suggestions for various changes to the passage, her idea for the book's title, and for her constant support of me and of my work. As with everything else in my life, this, too, was made better because of her touch.

Foreword

One of the most fascinating things in this world in which we live is words...the spoken word...the written word...the word we hear...the word we read. Words have always moved people...they've moved nations...they've moved the world...I think the words on the pages to follow will move you.

Christopher Neck has written and compiled some of the most inspirational and motivational words that will ever grace us all. These words have come from all walks of life...from all races...from all religions. They are a tribute to the human spirit and what is great about life. This is the kind of work that will draw you close to past emotions...and find you turning to pages for future ones.

On words, Wilfred Peterson once wrote, "The art of words is to use them creatively; to select and arrange them to inspire the mind, stir the heart, lift the spirit...Words of power burst in man's mind with a great light, to illuminate his thoughts and show him the way...Choose well your words! They will go marching down the years in the lives you touch."

So enjoy the journey as you travel through the pages to follow, for as you will learn, "It is the journey, not the destination," that counts.

Dale Brown
Head Basketball Coach
Louisiana State University
April 28, 1995

Introduction

The New Webster's Dictionary (1992) defines disease as "an unhealthy condition." Through the course of my teaching at the university level as well as training employees at various organizations, I have noticed a widespread epidemic that cannot be found in any medical journal or textbook - that is, the "unhealthy condition" that alters people's mental states in such a way that they believe they must settle for mediocrity in their lives. In other words, this "disease" leads beautiful human beings from all walks of life (e.g., homemakers, students, secretaries, managers, lawyers, etc.) toward putting their dreams in a box and sticking this box in an attic somewhere - to be forgotten. Goals such as writing a novel, beginning a business, going back to school, or traveling around the world get stored away forever, never taken out to be lived.

What causes this "disease" you might ask? Well, human behavior can be very complex, but what I've found through talking with my students and clients is that they've succumbed to this dreaded mental condition via different routes. Some have experienced failure many times in their lives and have just stopped trying. Others have swayed away from their dreams by pressure from well-meaning friends and family members to pursue a specific direction, even though it wasn't their "calling." As one student told me, "I'm going to law school because my dad's a lawyer; but what I really want to do is to teach at the high school level." Still, some inflicted by this "disease" just have never been fortunate enough to have someone to encourage them, to convince them that they could do whatever they wanted with their lives - that they could make a difference. Consequently, this lack of support creates a situation where these individuals don't believe they are capable of achieving their grandest ideals.

Just as researchers develop "drugs" to stop the spreading of medical diseases, I felt it was necessary to develop a "natural" medicine to combat this disease that zaps people's dream attainment. Medicine for the Mind is such a remedy. The seeds for this book were planted approximately seven years ago. I realized that many of my students and clients were suffering from this "mediocrity" thinking. So, in order to make my students and clients examine their mental states, I began to compose simple, yet compelling stories and poems to read to them at the end of every class or training session. Additionally, I would always begin a learning session with a paralleling quote. I discovered that many people asked for copies of these because the words related to their lives and gave them hope for their dreams. After six years of teaching and training thousands of individuals, these stories, poems, and quotes began to grow in number. I felt that if my students and clients were benefiting from these words, then maybe others could benefit also. Consequently, <u>Medicine for the Mind</u> is a compilation of the "best" stories, poems, and quotes.

The inspirational poems, stories, and quotes in <u>Medicine for the Mind</u> will hopefully help you to either cure yourself of this dreadful disease or to help you prevent it from ever occurring within you. <u>Medicine for the Mind</u> is broken down into various sections to help restore you to health...to a state where you believe you can achieve whatever you desire. These sections include: Take the First Step, Mental Power, The Will to Prepare, Hard Work, Picking Yourself Up, Who Am I? and Helping Others.

Each section offers you a different form of medicine - that is, unique information for you to absorb to help you reach your ultimate potential. The prescription dosage for the medicine in this book is up to you. Read as much as you need whenever you feel that you need some "healing" words to keep your dreams and goals alive.

Nikos Kazantzakis once wrote:

> Ideal teachers are those who use themselves as bridges over which they invite their students to cross; then having facilitated their crossing, joyfully collapse, encouraging them to create bridges of their own.

I invite you now to cross over into the inspirational words of this book. My sincere hope is that the poems, stories, and quotes in <u>Medicine for the Mind</u> will inspire you to create your own "bridges" to your dreams.

- Christopher P. Neck, Ph.D. -

x

The Author

Dr. Christopher P. Neck completed his Ph.D. in Management at Arizona State University. He is currently an Associate Professor of Management at Virginia Polytechnic Institute and State University (popularly known as Virginia Tech). He received his M.B.A. from Louisiana State University. Neck is author of the books Fit To Lead: The Proven 8-week Solution for Shaping Up Your Body, Your Mind, and Your Career (2004, St. Martin's Press), Mastering Self-Leadership: Empowering Yourself for Personal Excellence, 4rd edition, (2007, Prentice-Hall), The Wisdom of Solomon at Work (2001, Berrett-Koehler), , For Team Members Only: Making Your Workplace Team Productive and Hassle-Free (1997, Amacom Books), and Medicine for the Mind: Healing Words to Help You Soar, 2nd Edition (McGraw-Hill, 2007).

Dr. Neck's research specialties include employee/executive fitness, self-leadership, leadership, group decision-making processes, and self-managing teams. He has over seventy publications in the form of books, chapters, and articles in various journals. Some of the outlets in which Neck's work has appeared include Organizational Behavior and Human Decision Processes, The Journal of Organizational Behavior, The Academy of Management Executive, Journal of Applied Behavioral Science, The Journal of Managerial Psychology, Executive Excellence, Human Relations, Human Resource Development Quarterly, Journal of Leadership Studies, Educational Leadership, and The Commercial Law Journal.

Due to Neck's expertise in management, he has been cited in numerous national publications including The Washington Post, The Wall Street Journal, The Los Angeles Times, The Houston Chronicle, and the Chicago Tribune, Additionally, Neck teaches a management practices course to a single class of over 1000 students at Virginia Tech. He has received numerous teaching awards at Virginia Tech, including the 2002 Wine Award for Teaching Excellence. Also, Neck is the seven time winner (1996, 1998, 2000, 2002, 2004, 2005, 2006) of the "Students' Choice Teacher of The Year Award" (voted by the students for the best teacher of the year within the entire university). Also, some of the organizations who have participated in Neck's management development training include GE/Toshiba, Busch Gardens, Clark Construction, the United States Army, Crestar, American Family Insurance, Sales and Marketing Executives International, America West Airlines, American Electric Power, W. L. Gore & Associates, Dillard's Department Stores, and Prudential Life Insurance. Neck is also an avid runner. He has completed 12 marathons, including the Boston Marathon, New York City Marathon, and the San Diego Marathon. In fact, he recently set a personal record for a single long distance run---a 32.6 mile run.

1

Take the First Step

Have you ever said to yourself, "Someday I'll?" Someday I'll start studying harder...Someday I'll take that vacation to Europe...Someday I'll start my own business...Someday I'll begin that exercise program...Someday I'll begin that novel. Someday when the bills are paid, when the semester is over, when I get out of school, when I have more time, when the kids are out of the house, then I'll start making progress toward my dreams. Do you have any someday I'll's? The problem with someday I'll's is that they never come. Someday I'll's end up in a pile of unfulfilled goals and dreams, and wasted potential. If you wait until all the signals are green to begin striving to obtain your ultimate desires, they will die because there will never be a "perfect" time to start. Life is precious, so the time to begin achieving your dreams is right now. The hardest part many times for achieving your goals is that first step. So take it. Begin now...Seize the day!

START YOUR SOMEDAYS...TODAY!

Have you ever put something off
Because the timing wasn't just exact?
Maybe you refused to take that first step
As fear stopped you in your tracks.

How about refusing to begin your dreams,
Putting things off for a while.
Have you ever said, "Maybe tomorrow?"
Have you ever said, "Someday I'll?"

Consider the intelligent lady
With the ability to make good grades.
She said she'd further her education
Once the bills were paid.

Or how about the older gentleman
Who wanted to travel the world around.
He said he'd begin his journey
Once his schedule began to slow down.

What about the aspiring young lad
Who had that novel written - in his mind.
He said he'd put it on paper
Whenever he could possibly find the time.

And finally, that love-struck person
With secret admiration for that guy..
She would let him know her true feelings
When she wasn't feeling all that shy.

The message of these examples,
I hope, is crystal clear.
The time to start your aspirations
Is now - not next year.

Because the bills might never get paid,
Your schedule won't slow down,
Extra time won't somehow appear,
Complete confidence won't be found.

So if you wait to take all those risks
Until all the signals say, "Go,"
Your "someday I'lls" will never come;
Your dreams, you'll never know.

So begin that job or go back to school.
Start to smile and remove that frown.
"Because sometimes you have to jump off that cliff;
And build your wings - on the way down."

ৡ

Twenty years from now you will be more disappointed by the things that you didn't do than by the ones you did do. So throw off the bowlines. Sail away form the safe harbor. Catch the trade winds in your sails. Explore. Dream. Discover."

- Mark Twain -

Do all you can with what you have, in the time you have, in the place you are.
- Nkosi Johnson -

To do anything in the world
worth doing, we must not
stand back shivering and
thinking of the cold and danger,
but jump in and scramble
through as well as we can.
                    - Sydney Smith -

Action is
eloquence.

-William Shakespeare -

Apply yourself: Get all the education you can,
but then, by God, do something. Don't just
stand there, make it happen.
- Lee Iococca -

If we listened to our intellect, we'd never have a love affair. We'd
never have a friendship. We'd never go into business, because
we'd be cynical. Well that's nonsense. You've got to jump off
cliffs all the time and build your wings on the way down.

- Ray Bradbury -

There came a time when the risk to remain tight in a bud was more painful than the risk it took to blossom.
- Anais Nin -

Don't just wish upon a star... be one!
- Unknown -

The great dividing line between success and failure can be expressed in five words, "I did not have time."

- Franklin Field -

❧

LEADING THE BAND

She was going to be the President
Of the U. S. of A.
He was going to become an actor
In a Broadway play.

As youngsters - these were their dreams;
The visions they aspired to.
They truly thought these aspirations,
Eventually, would one day come true.

But she did not become President.
The reason is the ultimate sin.
She never ran for office.
She feared she would not win.

He didn't make it to New York City.
In fact, never set a foot on the stage.
He thought he'd forget his lines.
In other words - he was afraid.

The lesson in these stories
Is that you must get up and try.
If you let your fears control you,
Your dreams will quickly die.

Because if you want to hit a home run,
You have to go up to the plate.
If you want to meet that special person,
You have to ask them for a date.

The biggest crime in life
Is to forget what you have dreamt.
It's not the act of losing
But to have never made the attempt.

So as you battle with your fears in life,
Remember this brief command:
"If you're not afraid to face the music,
You may one day lead the band."

❧

Ain't no
chance if
you don't
take it.
  - Guy Clark -

Of all sad words of tongue or
pen, the saddest are these:
"It might have been."
                    - J. G. Whittier -

THE BEST TIME TO PLANT
A TREE WAS 20 YEARS AGO.
THE SECOND BEST TIME IS NOW.
                    - Chinese Proverb -

That it will never come again
is what makes life so sweet.
                    - Emily Dickinson -

**One to-day is worth
two to-morrows.**
- Benjamin Franklin -

You only live once,
but if you work it
right, once is enough.
                    - Joe E. Lewis -

Don't be afraid your life
will end;
be afraid that it will
never begin.
                    - Grace Hansen -

Time is the least
thing we have....
- Ernest Hemingway -

12

♑

DREAMS ARE FOR THOSE WHO PURSUE

Sometimes when you feel that nothing's going your way,
And there's no way you'll achieve success;
You've reached that point where it's time to give up;
There's no way to be your best.

All hope is gone; you have nothing left;
You and your dreams must part.
This is the time to hear this story
And see how it touches your heart.

There was a farmer who was asked by his kids
To get some milk to drink.
The farmer was perplexed; he didn't know how.
So for days he tried to think.

Then presto like magic, it came to him.
His idea, he thought, was a plum.
He would sit on a stool in the middle of a field
And wait for the cow to come.

He waited and waited but never once
Did a cow back up to his nest.
So he called it quits and picked up his chair;
His kids were denied their request.

The moral of this quaint little tale
Is that your dreams won't come to you.
You must work really hard and always persist
If you want them one day to come true.

Success is for those who are willing to work;
The bottom line - it's up to you;
Sitting and waiting will get you nowhere
Because dreams are for those who pursue.

♑

> *You should plant your own garden instead of*
> *waiting for someone else to bring you flowers.*
> - Veronica Shoffstall -

XXXXXXXXXXXXXXXXXXXXXXXXXXXXXXXXXXXXXXXXX
Good things come to those who wait...however it is
usually that which has been left behind by those who
hustle.

- Abraham Lincoln -
XXXXXXXXXXXXXXXXXXXXXXXXXXXXXXXXXXXXXXXXX

> Even if you're on the right track,
> you'll get run over if you just sit there.
> - Will Rogers -

There are risks and costs to a program
of action. But they are far less than
the long range risks and costs of
comfortable inaction.
- John F. Kennedy -

He who has
begun has
half done.
Dare to be
wise; begin!

- Horace -
65-8 B.C.

THE PEOPLE WHO GET ON IN THIS WORLD ARE THE PEOPLE WHO GET UP AND LOOK FOR THE CIRCUMSTANCES THEY WANT, AND, IF THEY CAN'T FIND THEM, MAKE THEM.
- George Bernard Shaw -

You can't build a reputation
on what you're <u>going</u> to do.
- Henry Ford -

Inaction saps the vigor
of the mind.
- Leonardo Da Vinci -

16

SEIZE THE DAY

CARPE DIEM
Is what I say.
In other words,
Seize the day!

To make it simpler,
I will relay.
"Gather ye rosebuds,
While ye may."

Consider this simple scenario;
Ponder it for a while.
Hopefully, it will make you think
And maybe change your style.

If you were given two dozen golden coins
To spend each day you choose,
But when the day is up, the one's you didn't spend,
You'd completely lose,

Your actions in this situation
Shouldn't require you to stall.
Of course you would reply,
"I wouldn't save any at all."

In our real lives, this actually does occur.
This truly does transpire.
We're given 24 golden hours each day
To use any way we desire.

But many times we don't use them wisely;
Commonplace is how they appear.
We treat them as if we truly believe
We can save them for sometime next year.

But once the day is finished,
No matter your chosen endeavor,
No one can ever retrieve it.
An hour lost is gone forever.

The message in these basic words
Is don't waste your "coins" away.
Always give it all you've got.
Carpe Diem - Seize the Day!

Know the true value of time;
snatch, seize, and enjoy every
moment of it. No idleness, no laziness,
no procrastination; never put off til tomorrow
what you can do today.   - Lord Chesterfield -

Only put off until tomorrow what you are willing
to die having left undone.
- Pablo Picasso -

Some people wait so
long for their ship to
come in, their pier collapses.
- John Goddard -

Take time to deliberate;
but when the time for action
arrives, stop thinking and go in.
- Andrew Jackson -

Oh God, to reach the point of death
only to find that you never lived at all.
                    - Thoreau -

Yesterday is a canceled check;
tomorrow is a promissory note;
today is the only cash you have -
so spend it wisely.
                    - Kay Lyons -

Seize the day; put no
trust in the morrow!
                    - Horace -

I have realized that
the past and the future are real
illusions, that they exist only in the
present, which is what there is
and all that there is.
                    - Alan Watts -

⌘

DREAMS BEGIN WITH THE FIRST STEP

You know you can obtain your dream;
You feel it in your heart.
But, there's something blocking your way;
You don't know where to start.

You can see yourself in that ideal job
Or living along the beach.
But, since you don't know where to begin,
It almost seems out of reach.

Giving up is an option
Because you really don't know how.
What I am proposing right here -
The time to start is now.

Consider the most beautiful song in the world;
It puts a lump in your throat.
As touching as this melody might be,
It began with just one note.

What about the longest journey ever done;
After its completion, the explorer wept.
As inspiring as this accomplishment was,
It began with the very first step.

Or how about that brilliant novel
That really provoked your mind.
It wasn't written all at once
But rather, a chapter at a time.

As these examples should illustrate,
Those who aim really high
Attempt to make their dreams become real
By beginning with the very first try.

So write the first page, or play the first note,
Whatever goal you aspire to.
Because unless you take the initial step,
Your dreams will never come true.

⌘

the most brilliant symphony in the world began with just one note.
- Anonymous -

a journey of a thousand leagues begins with a single step.
- Lao-Tzu -

Whatever you can do or dream,
you can begin it.
Boldness has genius, power,
and magic in it.
- Goethe -

The key to happiness is having dreams -
the key to success is making them come true.
- Unknown -

**If you have built castles in the air, your work need not be lost;
that is where they should be. Now put foundations under
them.**
- Henry David Thoreau -

If you wish to soar with eagles, you must be willing to jump
off some cliffs.
- Unknown -

24

2

Mental Power

Puff, puff, chug, chug, went
the Little Blue Engine. "I think
I can - I think I can - I think I
can - I think I can - I...."
Up, up, up.
Faster and faster the little
engine climbed, until at last
they reached the top of the
mountain. And the little
Blue Engine smiled and
seemed to say as she puffed
steadily down the mountain.
"I thought I could. I thought I
could. I thought I could...."

- W. Piper, 1930 -

As children, many of us heard these words spoken by the Little Blue Engine, "I think I can, I think I can, I think I can, I think I can...." The Little Engine thought these words to herself to help her get over the mountain. In the same way, what you think to yourself can help you climb your own personal mountain to success. In short, your success in life begins in one place, that is - your mind. The way you think can be the catalyst toward the achievement of your grandest dreams. Your mind is so powerful that it has a significant impact on what you are experiencing right now. As Milton wrote, your mind "can make a Heaven of Hell; a Hell of Heaven." So if your life right now is not what you want it to be, the first place to begin is in your mind...in the way you think. If you are feeling "down," think "up." If you are "scared," think "courage." If you are really "stressed," think "relaxed." If you are suffering from low self-esteem, think "confidence." Once you begin to repeat these positive thoughts to yourself over and over again, your body will follow your mind's messages...and your "hell" will become your "heaven." So begin right now to use your mental power to help you succeed in the game of life.

👍

TURN YOUR WEAKNESSES INTO STRENGTHS

Have you ever felt sorry for yourself
Because you thought you possessed a flaw?
Maybe you weren't as smart or attractive
As someone else you saw?

Then listen to this simple story.
I hope that you will do
Because maybe it will change your mind
And alter your point of view.

There was a king whose source of power
Was a rare diamond, one of a kind.
But one day he dropped it; a scratch appeared.
The brilliant stone had lost its shine

He tried and tried to make it right
But the scratch would not go away.
An old man volunteered to give it a shot.
He would come back the very next day.

When the old man returned to the castle,
The king beamed like a radiant sun.
The diamond was now more stunning than ever.
And this is what the old man had done.

A beautiful rose was so elegantly carved
On the face of the gem.
And the ugly scratch that was once a flaw
Now served as the stem.

The moral of this quaint little tale
Is that by altering your frame of mind,
Your imperfections will no longer exist.
Success you soon will find.

Your faults can be your best assets
If you perceive them this way.
They can actually be the catalyst
Toward achievement everyday.

So don't dwell on what you don't have
Or ponder the "scratches" on you.
By turning your weaknesses into strengths,
Your dreams will one day come true.

Restlessness and discontent are the first necessities of progress.
- Thomas Edison -

Making the simple complicated is commonplace; making the complicated simple, awesomely simple, that's creativity.
- Charles Mingus -

IT'S SO EASY TO BE CYNICAL. IT'S MUCH HARDER, IT TAKES A PHILOSOPHICAL POINT OF VIEW, TO BE OPTIMISTIC. YOU HAVE TO WORK AT IT EVERY DAY.
-Yo-Yo Ma -

There are two ways to live your life.
One is as though nothing is a miracle.
The other is as though everything is a miracle.
- Albert Einstein -

It is not by regretting what is irreparable that true work is to be done, but by making the best of what we are. It is not by complaining that we have not the right tools, but by using well the tools we have... and the manly and the wise way is to look your disadvantages in the face, and see what can be made of them.

- Frederick N. Robertson -

A man is what he thinks about all day long.
- Ralph Waldo Emerson -

The wisest of insights that can be
gained by any man or woman is
the realization that our world is not
so much what it is but what we choose
it to be.
- Charles C. Manz -

Rule your mind or
it will rule you.
- Horace -

One's own thought is one's world.
What a person thinks is what he becomes -
That is the eternal mystery!
                              - Mastr. Upanishad -

All that we are	*The real voyage of discovery*
is the result of	*consists not in seeking*
what we have	*new landscapes, but in*
thought.	*having new eyes.*
- Buddha -	- Marcel Proust -

**The greatest discovery of my time is that human
beings can alter their lives by altering their attitudes.**
- William James -

HANDFULS OF GIFTS

In March of 1988, Helen Thayer was on a journey that few believed could be accomplished - a solo trek to the North magnetic Pole - a first for a woman. She had only one week left in her grueling exploration when an unexpected storm developed - blowing most of her remaining supplies away - except seven small handfuls of walnuts and a pint of water. Thus, she would have to adjust from living off 5,000 calories a day to 100 calories. Did she make it to her destination? Yes, she certainly did! How did she manage to finish her incredible feat? Her will to win and the power of her mind were her strategic weapons against the brutal elements - the wind, the cold, the man-eating polar bears. As Mrs. Thayer remarked in her book, <u>Polar Dream</u>, about her northern journey:

> I found it to be a decided advantage to accept what I had and feel grateful for it rather than wish I had more. Wishing only made me feel even more hungry and thirsty, whereas acceptance and gratitude allowed me to channel my energy into moving ahead at a good pace....

The lesson that Mrs. Thayer learned during her exploration can serve as a catalyst for each of us toward enhancing our own lives. Specifically, how many times during each day do we focus on what we don't have...If I only had a new car; if I only could win the lottery; if I only had a better job; if only I were married; if only I had more free time...rather than feeling blessed for the gifts that you do have. By accepting what we do have, we will be able to focus our energy toward moving in the direction of our goals. Wishing for something or complaining because you don't have something in your life is just wasted negative energy that distracts you from moving closer to your dreams. As Oliver Wendell Holmes once said, "I find the greatest thing in this world is not so much where we stand as in what direction we are moving." Wishing or complaining usually prevents any progression toward the direction of your choice. So while you are traveling along your life's journey toward reaching your potential and enjoying happiness, success, and inner peace, some unexpected storms might develop. These storms might at first look like insurmountable obstacles or barriers to preventing you from making your dreams reality. However, don't let these hardships prevent you from succeeding. Don't drown your mind with buckets of negative thought. Instead of thinking, "I could accomplish my goals if only these obstacles were not in my way," tell yourself, "These obstacles can only make me stronger. I do have what it takes to overcome these hardships. I will persevere and achieve my dreams; nothing can stop me." Gather all of your strength and plow full steam toward your aspirations. Remember to feel truly grateful for the blessings that you do have in your life...your health, your family, your parents, your children, your eyesight...remember to feel truly blessed for your handfuls of walnuts.

Everything can be taken from man except the last of the human freedoms, his ability to choose his own attitude in any given set of circumstances, to choose his own way. Remember this choice of attitude when you are feeling overwhelmed by your circumstances.

- Victor Frankl -

It may not be your
fault for being down,
but it's got to be
your fault for not
getting up.
- Steve Davis -

Impossible is a word to
be found only in the dictionary of fools.
- Napoléon Bonaparte -

A mind not to be changed by place or time,
the mind is its own place, and in itself can
make a Heaven of Hell, a Hell of Heaven.
- John Milton -

To see a World in a Grain of Sand
And a Heaven in a Wild Flower
Hold Infinity in the palm of your hand
And Eternity in an hour.
- William Blake -

YOU CAN IF YOU BELIEVE

The mind is an incredible instrument;
It can control who you are.
It can restrict you to mediocrity
Or make you a superstar.

It depends on how you think.
Do you place limitations on yourself?
Your thoughts affect your actions
In addition to your health.

The purpose of this story
Is to really get you to see
That if you can only imagine it,
It can become reality.

If you can vividly dream it,
See the picture in your mind,
Then one day you'll achieve it
And one day you will find

That by believing in your dreams,
Channeling all thoughts toward your goals,
You will one day become a success
Instead of one of those poor and desolate souls

Who never experiences victory
Because they're afraid to truly believe.
They settle for being only average;
Never once do they achieve.

So dream BIG, not small;
Don't let anything get in the way.
Dream of being president,
Of making the winning play.

Dream of rainbows; dream of gold;
Dream of reaching the highest peak;
Dream of sunsets; dream of oceans -
Whatever it is you might seek.

Dream of one day meeting your soul mate;
Dream of that house on the beach.
As long as you think you can,
Nothing is beyond your reach.

The secret is how you think;
It's the fuel for a superstar.
Positive thinking is high octane.
It will take you very far.

So don't waste another day
Of blaming others for your distress.
Just changing the way you think
Can turn your failure into success.

So think positive and dream BIG
And one day you will see -
As long as you think you can,
Then one day it will be.

If you can believe it, you can achieve it...
If you can dream it, you can become it.
                    - William A. Ward -

The Divinity that shapes our ends is in ourselves...
All that a man achieves or fails to achieve is the direct result of his own
thoughts.
                                        - James Lane Allen -

If you think you can, or you think you can't,
you're probably right.   - Mark Twain -

If you can dream it, you can
do it. Always remember that this
whole thing was started by a mouse.
                    - Walt Disney -

Aerodynamically the bumble bee shouldn't be able to fly, but the bumble bee doesn't know it so it goes on flying anyway.
- Mary Kay Ash -

Throughout the centuries there were those
who took first steps down new roads armed
with nothing but their own vision.
- Ayn Rand -

The minute you start talking
about what you're going to
do if you lose, you
have lost.
- George Shultz -

THE VISION

Do you have a grand idea
To which some might laugh and smile?
They think it can't be done;
They call it a "someday I'll."

Then consider this story of two men;
Their business was selling shoes.
They were confronted with the same situation,
But each had differing views.

Both were sent to a far-away island
To test if their abilities were elite.
And they discovered, upon arrival,
The natives had nothing on their feet.

The first sadly called his boss
With a very large case of despair,
Relayed that there was no hope for business
Because everyone's feet were bare.

The second was filled with much elation;
Told his superior the good news.
Said he was going to make a million.
No one *yet* was wearing shoes.

The meaning in these few words
Is your thoughts can help you advance
Because to what some might spell disaster
Could be for you, your one big chance.

The secret to creating opportunities
Isn't money or political pull.
Simply, it's your attitude -
Is the glass half-empty or half-full?

A different real world example
Might help reveal this story's key.
It's a lesson of a pollinating insect,
The plight of the bumble bee.

According to the laws of science,
The bee should not be able to fly.
But this creature didn't acknowledge this
And instead gave flight a try.

So remember what history reveals
As you pinpoint your dreams with precision;
The primary keys to greatness
Are your attitude and your vision.

<<<<<<<<<<<<<<<<<<<<<<<<<<<<<<<<<<>>>>>>>>>>>>>>>>>>>>>>>>>

A wise man will make more opportunities than he finds.
- Sir Francis Bacon -

<<<<<<<<<<<<<<<<<<<<<<<<<<<<<>>>>>>>>>>>>>>>>>>>>>>>>>

We are continually faced by great opportunities
brilliantly disguised as insoluble problems.
- Anonymous -

Opportunity is missed by most people because
it is dressed in overalls and looks like work.
- Thomas Edison -

Problems are only opportunities in work clothes.
- Henry J. Kaiser -

> The pessimist sees the difficulty in
> every opportunity; the optimist, the
> opportunity in every difficulty.
> - L. P. Jacks -

Nurture your mind with great thoughts,
for you will never go any higher than you think.
> - Benjamin Disraeli -

**Some men see things as they are and say,
"Why?"
I dream things that never were
and say,
"Why not?"**
- George Bernard Shaw -

I love those who yearn for the impossible.
- Johann Wolfgang Von Goethe -

CONQUERING THE UNKNOWN

Have you ever felt afraid?
All alone in the dark?
You needed a little push
Or maybe a fiery spark.

In your mind you had a vision
Of something you wanted to do.
But uncertainty was holding you back
From making this dream come true.

Then consider the high school graduate
With much potential to be found.
But she never tasted success;
She feared leaving her hometown.

Or the woman dreaming of the passionate marriage
With a man of much charm.
She settled for a comfortable relationship
Even though it was just lukewarm.

And finally that middle-aged manager
Dreaming of becoming an entrepreneur;
Yet, settled for his nine-to-five job
Because it was so secure.

The message in these scenarios
Is that you must prevent your fear
From paralyzing your ambitions,
From stifling your career.

This monster called "the unknown"
Can scare you into retreat;
Toward settling for mediocrity
And wailing in defeat.

So as you aspire to unlimited heights,
Fear might knock you to the floor.
But remember, "You can't discover new oceans
Unless you first lose sight of the shore."

Brooks become crooked from taking the path of least resistance.
So do people.
> - Harold E. Kohn -

---

*The important thing is this:
to be ready at any moment to
sacrifice what we are for what
we could become.*
> - Charles Dubois -

A ship is safe in harbor -
but that's not what ships
are for.
> - J. A. Shedd -

Don't be afraid to go out on a limb.
That's where the fruit is.
> - Soundings -

Man cannot discover new oceans unless
he
has courage to lose sight of the shore.
> - Andre Gide -

Security is mostly a superstition.
resistance
It does not exist in nature. Avoiding
and mastery
danger is no safer in the long run than
not
outright exposure. Life is either a daring
of fear.
adventure or nothing.

- Helen Keller -

If you always do what you've always done,
you'll always get what you've always gotten.
- Anonymous -

Unless you try to do something beyond what you
have already mastered, you will never grow.
- Ralph Waldo Emerson -

It must happen to us all...We pack up what we've learned so far
and leave the familiar behind. No fun, that shearing separation,
but somewhere within we must dimly know that saying good-bye
to safety brings the only security we'll ever know.
- Richard Bach -

We are enmeshed in the cancerous discipline of security. And in
the worship of security, we fling our lives beneath the wheels of
routine, and before we know it our lives are gone.
- Sterling Hayden -

3

The Will to Prepare

Imagine for a moment that you are at an airport with two jam-packed suitcases. You arrive at the ticket counter all excited and ready to go. However, when the ticketing agent asks you, "Where are you going?" you reply, "I'm not sure."

Does this sound silly? Possibly it does. However, when it comes to your life's travels, rather than an airplane ride, you might actually be acting like the person in the scenario above. In your life you might be traveling without a specific destination for where you want to go and who you want to become. As Harvey McKay said, "If you don't have a destination, you'll never get there." Thus, if you don't have a clear mental picture of your dreams or if you don't have a plan to achieve them, how can you ever live them? On the other hand, those individuals who actually achieve and live their dreams have a destination in mind before they set out on their journey. In other words, they develop specific and concrete short-term and long-term goals for themselves. They are constantly preparing themselves to achieve these self-set goals. So if you want to achieve your dreams, you must do the same. For all areas of your life, career, school, family, friends, develop a plan for success (e.g., specific goals) and then execute your plans. The choice is up to you. If you don't prepare a plan, you will just go around and around in circles and never get anywhere close to making your dreams a reality. Remember, everyone has a dream - not everyone obtains it. Why? Those who do achieve their dreams not only have the will to succeed but also have the will to prepare to succeed.

✿

AN EXERCISE FOR SUCCESS

Have you ever gone to an airport,
All excited and packed to go?
But when asked where you were flying,
You said, "I don't know?"

If you feel this could never happen,
Something to be dreaded,
Then answer the following question,
"Where's your life headed?"

If you don't have a clear picture
Of your goals and drives,
It's the same as boarding an airplane
Without knowing where it'll arrive.

So if you want to take the first step
Toward exacting your life's direction,
Then follow this simple exercise
To help you obtain perfection.

Take out a pencil and paper,
Write down what you'd like to get done,
What you'd like to achieve,
And what you'd like to become.

It doesn't matter the number of words,
Specificity is the key.
Be sure to include the "when's" and "how's,"
A clear picture you'll start to see.

A goal that is written out
Can truly help you persist
Because it gives you a detailed plan
Toward making your dreams exist.

Thus, if you want to succeed in life,
Take note and prepare.
Because if you don't have a destination,
You'll never get anywhere.

✿

When I am getting ready to reason with a man,

I spend one-third of my time thinking about myself

And what I am going to say,

And two-thirds about him and what he is going to say.

- Abraham Lincoln -

If you don't have a destination, you'll never get there.
- Harvey Mackay -

My interest is in the future
because I am going to spend
the rest of my life there.   - Charles Kettering -

Make no little plans.
They have no magic to stir men's blood.
Make big plans: aim high in hope and work.
- D. H. Burnham -

Goals are not only absolutely necessary to motivate us.
They are essential to really keep us alive.
- Robert Schuller -

Goals serve as a stimulus to life. They tend to tap the deeper resources and draw out of life its best. Where there are no goals, neither will there be significant accomplishments. There will only be existence.

- Anonymous -

You must know for which harbor you are headed if you are to catch the right wind to take you there.
- Seneca -

Goals can give you power in life. A person or an organization without a goal is powerless.
- Lewis Timberlake -

Winners make goals; losers make excuses.
- Anonymous -

It must be borne in mind that the tragedy of life doesn't lie in not reaching your goal. The tragedy lies in having no goal to reach. Not failure, but low aim is sin.

- Helmut Schmidt -

☆

THE WILL TO PREPARE

This is a little story
Of the choice between Great or Fair.
It's about Perseverance and Drive.
It's about the will to prepare.

There was a young man preparing to try
A grueling Marathon.
He told everyone he'd do anything
To go Above and Beyond.

But as badly as he wanted to complete
This fatiguing 26-mile run,
He only trained every once in a while;
Instead, he settled for fun.

And when race day finally came,
The gun went off with a spark.
But this man with the will to win
Dropped out at the half-way mark.

The moral of the quaint little tale
Is no matter what you try,
Unless you're willing to pay the price,
Your dream will quickly die.

The choice is up to you.
If you want to be Great - not Fair,
The will to win is not enough.
Also needed is the WILL TO PREPARE.

> The will to win is not nearly important as the will to prepare to win.
>
> - Bobby Knight -

> Preparation
>   is a
> Prerequisite
>   to Success.   - Christopher Neck -

> Before everything else,
> getting ready is the
> secret of success.
> - Henry Ford -

> Remember, it wasn't
> raining when Noah
> built the ark.
>   - Howard Ruff -

Most people don't plan to fail, they fail to plan.
- John L. Beckley -

The secret of success in
life: Prepare for opportunity
when it comes.
- Benjamin Disraeli -

Practice does not make perfect;
perfect practice makes perfect.
- Vince Lombardi -

☹

NO SECOND CHANCES

Are you on your way to the top?
You think that you can't fail.
Before you go any further,
Let's examine a crucial detail.

Consider the jobless graduate
Who didn't know what to do.
So he decided to apply for a position;
Off he went to the interview.

His resume was quite impressive
With credentials so unique.
But he didn't get the job;
There was a flaw in his technique.

His attire was quite messy,
And he came across as meek
Because his eye contact meandered
And his handshake was too weak.

The moral of this story is
A product can be grandeur
But if it isn't packaged nicely,
It might never leave the store.

So as you continue your quest toward success,
Remember this simple lesson -
You might never get a second chance
To make a first impression.

First impressions can last a lifetime, so always be prepared.
- Anonymous -

We are all salesmen in the business of life.
Everyday we must sell a very special
product - ourselves.
- C. Neck -

**You don't have just one chance to win,
but you don't have unlimited opportunities either.**
- A. L. Williams -

Unless a person has trained himself for his chance,
the chance will only make him ridiculous. A great
occasion is worth to man exactly what his preparation
enables him to make of it.
- J.B. Matthews -

To be prepared
is half the victory.
- Miguel Cervantes -

4

Hard Work

A common definition for the word "work" is "physical or mental effort directed toward a goal." The two key words in this definition are "effort" and "goal." If you want to make your dreams and goals a reality, you must exert effort. If you want to complete that college degree, start your own business, meet your future husband/wife, complete that novel, you must produce some sweat - that is, work hard. The people who experience the exhilaration of "achievement" are those who work hard rather than waiting for "lady luck" to bring their dreams to them. Because when it comes to dreams, there are no handouts, no shortcuts, and no free lunches. Success is not a give away or something you win over the phone. Rather, it is the result of many hours, days, months, and years of persistent effort. As Patrick Riley once said, "Hard work won't guarantee you a thing, but without it, you don't stand a chance." So, give yourself a solid chance toward achieving your dreams by working hard.

THE PRICE OF SUCCESS

The woman was quite perplexed.
She had failed to make C.E.O.
Why was she passed over for the position?
She really wanted to know.

The young man sat teary-eyed.
Why didn't he qualify for the Olympic Team?
Ever since he was a little kid,
This had always been his dream.

But if we explore a little further,
The reason is simply a crime.
These people fell short of their aspirations
Because they didn't put in the time.

The woman worked only from nine to five;
Every weekend slowed her stride.
The young man trained only in pleasant weather;
On rainy days, he stayed inside.

But, there is some beauty in these failures;
It's that from them, you can learn
That winning is not a handout,
Success, you must earn.

To be the best in what you do
Does not come easily.
The prescription is straightforward;
Hard work is the key.

So if you want to achieve your potential in life,
Remember this simple perk:
"The dictionary is the only place
that <u>success</u> comes before <u>work</u>.

▲

For most of us, health will depend not on who we are, but on how we live. The body you have at 20 depends on your genes, but the body you have at 40, 60, or 80 is the body you deserve, the body that reflects your behavior. — Harvey B. Simon, M.D. -

A FIELD THAT IS RESTED GIVES A BOUNTIFUL CROP.
- Ovid -

Do not confuse motion and progress. A rocking horse keeps moving but does not make any progress.
- Alfred A. Montapert -

You never know how a horse will pull until you hook him to a heavy load.
- Coach Bear Bryant -

Complete Abstinence is easier than perfect moderation.
- St. Augustine -

The really idle man gets nowhere.
The perpetually busy man does not get much further.
- Sir Heneage Ogilvie -

CHOP YOUR OWN WOOD, AND IT WILL WARM YOU TWICE.
- Henry Ford -

Hard work won't guarantee
you a thing
but without it,
you don't stand a chance.
- Patrick Riley -

I do not want to convince
my son that someone will guarantee
him a living. I want him rather
to realize that there is plenty
of opportunity in this country for
him to achieve success, but whether
he wins or loses depends entirely
on his own character, perseverance,
thrift, intelligence and capacity
for hard work.
- Major John L. Griffith -

What is happening to our drive, to our
spirit, to our initiative? This morning, I
saw two robins standing in line for worm stamps.

- Bob Orben -

**Look at a day when you are supremely satisfied at the end.
It's not a day when you lounge around doing nothing.
It's when you've had everything to do, and you've done it.**
- Margaret Thatcher -

Rules for business success:
work hard and you will
succeed.
- Rothschild -

There's a difference between interest and commitment.
When you're interested in doing something, you do it
only when circumstances permit. When you're
committed to something, you accept no excuses, only results.

- Art Turock -

C☪

WORK: THE BEST LUCKY CHARM

There is a fortuitous word
Defined by Webster in this stance.
A "random occurrence of fortune,"
Or just simply "chance."

This term that's in the spotlight
Is one you've heard before;
One that many people rely on
To help them truly soar.

Can you guess this noun in question?
Possibly you might be stuck
In case you can't derive it,
This word is known as "<u>luck</u>."

Consider the man of 30 years,
When asked what he wanted to behold,
Said he wanted to make much money -
A huge portfolio.

He continued to elaborate
A plan "up his sleeve" he had.
He'd put his faith in the lottery;
That would be his launch pad.

Every week he bought a ticket
And patiently waited to see
If the numbers he had chosen
Appeared on his TV.

But after ten long years,
Fortune never came his way.
He wasn't the big winner;
Lady Luck didn't pay.

He decided to change his approach;
One that deep down he knew he could believe.
He opened his own restaurant -
A method not so naive.

And instead of betting on randomness,
He acted as if on a crusade
Hoping his focused effort
Would lead him to his parade.

After five hard-working years
During which vacations were rare,
People were lining up for his cuisine,
The food of a millionaire.

The point to this little story
Is that your dreams might run amok
If you take the passive method
And solely rely on luck.

Because once you let fate lead the way,
It can begin to deter.
Success is not within your power,
A fluke event must occur.

So take destiny in your hands
And remember as you advance -
Hard work is no guarantee
But without it, you don't stand a chance.

☪

> **He who labors diligently
> need never despair;
> for all things are accomplished
> by diligence and labor.**
> - Menander -

> The three great essentials
> to achieve anything worthwhile
> are, first hard work; second,
> stick-to-itiveness;
> third, common sense.
> - Thomas Edison -

> I never knew a person who
> suffered from overwork. There
> are many, however, who suffered
> from too much ambition, and not enough action.
> - Dr. James Mantague -

Luck is what happens when preparation meets opportunity.
- Elmer Letterman -

About the only thing that comes without effort is old age.
- Unknown -

The record of historical achievement cries out in loud, condemning tones against laziness. Gibbon spent twenty-six years writing The Decline and Fall of the Roman Empire. Milton used to rise at four o'clock every morning in writing Paradise Lost. Bryant rewrote one of his essays ninety-nine times. Webster worked thirty-six years to produce the first edition of the dictionary that bears his name. Cicero practiced speaking before friends every day for thirty years to perfect his elocution.
- Help and Food -

NO SHORTCUTS

There was a little boy
Who loved to eat ice cream - everyday.
He'd travel for miles and miles
In his sleep, he knew the way.

But the route to his favorite dessert
Was not an easy one to begin.
It was full of hills and rocks
Requiring much energy to ascend.

So one day he took a detour
To reduce his travel time,
But along this shortcut he navigated,
The ice cream store, he didn't find.

What he found was a dead end.
The lad was lost and all alone.
He should have taken the difficult jaunt
Between his goal and his home.

The moral of this tiny tale,
I hope is clean and neat.
That traveling the road to success
Will not be an easy feat.

In fact, it will be quite difficult
With obstacles around each turn.
But if you attempt to overcome them,
You will eventually learn

That if you try to cut corners
As you strive to be supreme,
You'll end up in some lonely place,
Far away from your dream.

So as you soar toward the clouds,
It might help in always knowing,
There are not any shortcuts
To any place - worth going.

If you find a path with no obstacles,
it probably doesn't lead anywhere.
                              - Frank A. Clark -

Genius is one percent inspiration
and ninety-nine percent perspiration.
                              - Thomas Edison -

Everybody wants to go to heaven,
but nobody wants to die.
                              - Joe Louis -

All noble things are as
difficult as they are rare.
                              - Spinoza -

It is a funny thing about life; if you refuse
to accept anything but the best,
you very often get it.
- Somerset Maugham -

**There is no substitute
for hard work.**
- Thomas Edison -

You may have the loftiest
goals, the highest ideals,
the noblest dreams, but
remember this, nothing
works unless you do.
- Nido Qubein -

↗ ↘

NO LONG LINES

Dreams. The American Heritage Dictionary defines a dream as "an aspiration; an ambition." Some people dream of winning the lottery, becoming a movie star, or meeting their true love. One of my aspirations has always been to have thousands of people come to hear me speak...to motivate an arena of people to reach their potential, to be the catalyst toward helping masses of individuals achieve their dreams.

From the time I was a young child, I always strived to accomplish things that very few people could. The goals that I set for myself were always extremely lofty. I tried to accomplish things that could only be achieved through hard work and discipline. At the age of 15, I ran my first marathon. Six months before I ran this 26.2 mile race, I remember telling my mom that the daily training, anywhere from 8 to 20 miles, was tough. She remarked, "Chris, there aren't any long lines." When I asked her to explain, she said, "In order to be the best at something, to accomplish great tasks, it takes much hard work and perseverance. As a result, only a few special individuals are going to be willing to put forth the effort that it takes to enjoy success. Many who start will fall by the wayside. If dreams were easy to obtain, there would be a long line of people waiting to receive their dreams. But dreams are not handed out; you have to be willing to pay the price of hard work in order to obtain your aspirations."

At the age of 26, I began the grueling task of obtaining my Ph.D. One night during the middle of the program, I made a long distance phone call to my mom. I was tired of working 18 hours a day, seven days a week. In fact, I was questioning whether it was worth it or not. I was seriously considering dropping out of the doctoral program. When I heard my mom's voice, I immediately became teary-eyed. I told her what I was feeling and what I was thinking of doing. She told me she would support any decision I would make; however, she wanted me to remember one thing. She said, "Chris, remember, there aren't any long lines." After we hung up, I let these words saturate my thoughts. I knew she was right. I knew that I must continue working diligently to finish. It would be worth it in the end. I didn't drop out of the program. Two years later, I completed my Ph.D.

Today was a special day. It was special for two reasons. First, it was my 30th birthday. Second, a few hours ago, I accomplished my life-long dream. I spoke to 14,000 people at a university in Louisiana on how to conquer the boulders to success. My presentation went so well that the crowd gave me a standing ovation for over 10 minutes.

However, before I went on stage I was so nervous that I could barely swallow. Although I had given this same speech to many groups before, tonight seemed different. Never before had I spoken to such a large crowd. Doubts began to enter my mind. Would I captivate their attention? Would they receive the message of what I was trying to say? With only 10 minutes before I walked on stage, I was sitting in the dressing room sweating profusely. I felt like I couldn't breathe. For a moment, I felt like I could not go out there and face the thousands of people. Then, all of a sudden, there was a knock on the dressing room door. One of the stage hands walked in and handed me an envelope. I thanked him and closed the door. I sat down on the wooden bench and gently opened the envelope. Inside was a note with only a few simple words. It said, "Chris, there aren't any long lines. Love, Mom."

↗ ↘

The heights

of great men

reached and kept;

were not

attached

by sudden flight;

But they,

while companions

slept,

were toiling

upward

in the night.

- Henry Wadsworth Longfellow -

♣

THE BEST THINGS IN LIFE AREN'T FREE

He wanted to be a Doctor,
Or a Lawyer in D. C.
A Famous Jazz Guitarist,
Or maybe a Parent of Three.

He had heard the nonsense about hard work,
But he found a short-cut to his best.
He thought he could cut a few corners
To reach the place known as Success.

These short-cuts he called a Free Lunch,
Hand-outs he knew of a few.
He topped it off with several Give-Aways;
He knew his Dreams would come true.

But his ambitions never materialized
Because as he climbed Success's Ladder,
He found he was taking himself for a ride.
His Dreams weren't handed out on a platter.

He discovered that Lunches are not Free
And, the only Hand-Out was his own.
Success was not a Give-Away
Or something he won on the phone.

Rather, he uncovered a striking lesson
To his fantasies, he found the Key;
That exertion is the answer
And the best things in life aren't free.

Thus, as you ascend to your peak in life,
WORK HARD - don't despair!
And remember the person on the mountain top
Wasn't
    just
        placed
           there.

♣

The dictionary is the only place that success comes before work.
Hard work is the price we must pay for success.
I think you can accomplish almost anything if you're willing to pay the price.

- Vince Lombardi -

If people knew how hard I have had to work to gain mastery, it wouldn't seem so wonderful at all.

- Michelangelo -

I am a great believer
in luck,
and I find the harder I
work,
the more I have of it.
- Stephen Leacock -

Success is simply a matter of luck. Ask any failure.
- Unknown -

WHEN WE DO MORE THAN WE ARE
PAID TO DO, EVENTUALLY WE
WILL BE PAID MORE FOR WHAT WE DO.
- Zig Ziglar -

5

Picking Yourself Up

Sometimes the road to success appears to be paved by natural talent and perfect performances. But this is a myth, an illusion. People who succeed usually do so after many failed attempts. Show me a multi-millionaire, and I'll show you someone who at some point in his/her life was near bankruptcy. Show me an Academy Award winner, and I'll show you an actor or actress who at some point in his/her life was told to pursue another line of work. Show me an Olympic track star, and I'll show you someone who probably once dropped out of a race. Throughout history, people who accomplish the highest achievements have possessed something even more valuable than raw, natural talent. They have possessed a relentless will to succeed, to persist against all odds. If you want to successfully climb your personal mountain, whatever it might be, don't base your dreams on never taking a risk, on never falling on your face. Rather, determine that you will succeed no matter how many times you fall. As Mary Pickford remarked, "There is always another chance...this thing we call failure is not the falling down but the staying down." So don't ever stay down, don't ever give up, don't ever quit. Be persistent because achievement of your goal may be just around the corner.

SUCCESS DOES NOT MEAN NEVER FAILING!

Listen very closely
To a simple tale.
It's about picking yourself up,
About not being afraid to fail.

Have you ever been dejected
Because you didn't achieve success?
You fell just short of your goal,
Although you gave your best.

Then consider these little stories
Of greatness, large and small.
Of how successful people
Rise every time they fall.

Babe Ruth, the baseball superstar,
The greatest slugger, some may boast.
But he holds another record,
Of striking out the most.

And consider the writer, John Creasily,
Author of 500 manuscripts.
Before one of his books was published,
He received 700 rejection slips.

And finally, Abraham Lincoln,
The five dollar bill bears his name.
Before his presidential election,
He lost in seven other campaigns.

The moral of these examples
Should be clear to all,
That before the rainbow appears,
There's usually some rainfall.

So as you travel this journey of life,
It might sometimes help to recall,
Success is not in never failing
But in rising every time you fall.

As you go along your road in life, you will, if you aim high enough, also meet resistance.....but no matter how tough the opposition may seem, have courage still----and persevere.

- Madeleine Albright -

If you make a choice that doesn't please your mate, friends, or whoever, the world will not fall apart.

- Oprah Winfrey -

THE MOMENT AVOIDING FAILURE BECOMES YOUR MOTIVATOR, YOU'RE DOWN THE PATH OF INACTIVITY. YOU STUMBLE, ONLY IF YOU'RE MOVING.

-Roberto Goizueta -

IT IS NOT THE STRONGEST OF THE SPECIES THAT SURVIVE, NOR THE MOST INTELLIGENT, BUT THE ONE THAT IS MOST RESPONSIVE TO CHANGE.

- Charles Darwin -

96

Success is measured by endeavors;
the only real failure is a person who
does not try.
- Unknown -

Failure is good. It's fertilizer.
Everything I've learned about
coaching, I've learned from
making mistakes.
- Rick Pitino -

The freedom to fail
is vital if you're
going to succeed.
- Michael Korda -

Failure is the first step toward success.
- Confucius -

**There is always another chance...
This thing that we call
'failure' is not the falling down,
but the staying down.**
- Mary Pickford -

**There isn't much thrill to success
unless one had first been close to failure.**
- William Fealte -

*Failure is the opportunity
to begin more intelligently.*
- Henry Ford -

THE CLIMB TO THE TOP

There is a myth in this world.
In fact, it's more of a tale.
It argues that successful people
Don't ever really fail.

It's time to destroy this point of view
Because it's totally untrue.
The truth is that ambitious people
Fail just like me and you.

If you show me a multi-millionaire
With cash flowing all the time.
I bet at some point in her life,
She was destitute, without a dime.

And show me a renowned scientist,
One of the world's best.
Probably during his education
Failed to pass a test.

And finally, the world-class athlete,
Wearing the gold medal that he dreamt,
Was once told he wasn't good enough
To even make the attempt.

The point to all these examples
Is that successful people do fall.
They confront their share of obstacles
As they strive to attain it all.

Individuals who seek to live their dreams
Know what it's like to hit the ground.
But they know that if they persevere,
Nothing can keep them down.

The key is not in never failing,
But the action that follows next.
Successful people get right back up.
They don't stay down perplexed.

So as you strive to reach your ultimate peak,
Remember this little rhyme.
"If there were not any valleys,
There would be no mountains to climb."

Shoot for the moon.
Even if you miss it you
will land among the stars.
- Les Brown -

**There is the greatest
practical benefit in making
a few failures early in life.**
- T.H. Huxley -

The people who are really
failures are the people
who set their standards so low,
keep the bar at such a safe level,
that they never run the risk of failure.
- Robert Schuller -

I hope someday
to have so much
of what the world calls success,
that people will ask me,
"What's your secret?"
and I will tell them,
"I just get up again
when I fall down."
- Paul Harvey -

Be like a postage stamp.
Stick to something until you get there.
- Josh Billings -

**You never really lose until
you quit trying.**
- Mike Ditka -

✈

CATCHING THE WIND

There is a simple word
That you frequently hear.
It's the secret to success.
This word is "persevere."

If you look it up in the dictionary
To find the spelling and its gist.
Its message is quite simplistic.
It means...to persist.

To clarify the essence
Of what this verb relays,
Then listen to this story,
See what it has to say.

There was a quite young lad,
Given a sailboat for a gift.
So he headed out to the beach
With enthusiasm and his skiff.

After hours and hours of trying
And struggling with all his might,
The boat never really moved.
He just couldn't get it right.

But the young boy didn't give up.
He kept on doing his best.
In his mind he knew it would happen.
He'd be successful in his quest.

Then an amazing thing occurred.
You could tell by his expanding grin.
The vessel glided across the ocean.
He had finally caught the wind.

The message in this nautical ode
Is that in order to prevail
When hardships occur in your life,
You should never take down the sail.

If you want to achieve your goals,
To reach your lofty dream,
You must persist no matter what the odds,
Despite how hard it might seem.

So, as you negotiate the hurdles to success,
Remember again and again -
If you never quit and persevere,
One day you'll catch the wind.

✈

Never give up.
You can make it no
matter what comes.
Nothing worth having
is ever achieved
without a struggle.
- M. W. Edelman -

It isn't making mistakes that's critical;
it's correcting them and getting on
with the principal task.
- Donald Rumsfeld -

Big shots are only little shots
who keep shooting.
- Christopher Morley -

> Great works
>   are performed
>   not by strength,
>   but by perseverance.
>   - Samuel Johnson -

> It's a little like wrestling
> a gorilla. You don't quit
> when you're tired - you quit
> when the gorilla is tired.
>   - Robert Strauss -

> I think the secret to success in any field—whether it's fitness,
> health or longevity—is discipline. Discipline with your diet,
> discipline with your weight, discipline with your daily habits,
> discipline with your exercise.
>   - Dr. Kenneth Cooper -

☞

THE ROAD TO SUCCESS

Have you ever set a goal?
Planned it through and through?
But things didn't go as expected;
You were confused about what to do.

Your plan failed to proceed smoothly.
Obstacles blocked your path.
Giving up entered your mind
As success slipped from your grasp.

If these words ring a bell
Or make you teary-eyed,
Then listen very closely,
They might spark something inside.

There once was a mother and a father
In a family of five.
They were going to take their children
On a cross-country drive.

Before the journey began,
They carefully planned it out.
With a map and a compass,
They plotted the one best route.

But after only a few days of driving
On the highway they had chose,
Suddenly appeared a sign;
It said, "This road is closed."

So they took a little detour
From the plot that they had picked;
But heavy congestion soon approached.
The street was being fixed.

After waiting just a little while
Without a shout or tear,
The cars began to move on;
The traffic began to clear.

The message should be plain and true
In this simple ode:
Success is not an easy ride
And hardly a smooth road.

No matter how well you forecast,
Obstacles will always impede.
So just alter your plan and don't give up,
Eventually, you'll succeed.

Thus, in order to reach your potential,
To avoid your dream's destruction,
Remember, the road to success
Is always under construction.

☞

One who gains strength by overcoming
obstacles possesses the only strength
which can overcome adversity.
- Albert Schweitzer -

A man of character finds a special
attractiveness in difficulty,
since it is only by coming to grips
with difficulty that he can realize
his potentialities.
- Charles DeGaulle -

The difference between a successful person and others
is not a lack of strength, not a lack of knowledge, but rather in a lack of will.
- Vince T. Lombardi -

The people who get on in this world are
the people who get up and look for the
circumstances they want,
and, if they can't find them, make them.
- George Bernard Shaw -

You may not be able to control the wind
but you certainly can adjust the sails....
- Unknown -

It is a rough road that
leads to the heights of greatness.
- Seneca -

※

LET ME IN, COACH...I'M NOT TIRED

Have you ever had a setback,
Possibly was not the one hired?
That's no excuse to give up,
LET ME IN, COACH...I'M NOT TIRED.

You studied hard for that exam.
There was no way it could be.
On the front of your returned paper
Was the average grade of "C."

But this is not the time to pack up.
Rather, it's the time to be inspired.
Roll up your sleeves and bare down,
LET ME IN, COACH...I'M NOT TIRED.

You finally got the courage
To ask her out to dine.
She looked you straight in the eye
And gave you her best line.

Does this make you question yourself?
No way - be a die-hard.
Just give it another shot sometime,
LET ME IN, COACH...I'M NOT TIRED.

Let me in, Coach...I'm not tired.
What is this supposed to show?
It should serve as a reminder
Of what to do when you're feeling low.

In the football game of life,
It's the fourth quarter, your score is down.
Do you get ready to go back in?
Or do you just sit right on the ground?

Do you reach for all your reserves
Instead of saving them for another day?
Do you go sit on the bench?
Or let the coach know you're ready to play?

When obstacles won't let go of you,
And stare you in the face,
It's time to give it that little extra;
It's time to pick up your pace.

Others will stop and give up.
They won't go another inch.
They'll let the hurdles of life,
Send them straight to the bench.

So when you think failure has beaten you and won.
And your chance for success has expired,
Just reach down deep and keep telling yourself,
LET ME IN, COACH...I'M NOT TIRED.

❋

To get where you want to go,
you must keep on keeping on.
- Norman Vincent Peale -

When nothing seems to help,
I go and look at a stonecutter
hammering away at his rock,
perhaps a hundred times
without as much as a crack
showing in it.
Yet, at the hundred and first blow,
it will split in two,
and I know it was not
that blow that did it, but
all that had gone before.
- Jacob A. Riis -

Perseverance is a great element of success.
If you only knock long enough and loud
enough at the gate, you are sure to wake up somebody.
- Henry Wadsworth Longfellow -

By perseverance,
the snail reached
the ark.
- Charles H. Spurgeon -

Growing is like running
a twenty-six mile marathon.
If we give up on the
twenty-fourth mile,
we will never know what
it feels like to finish the race.
- Anonymous -

SHAME AND POVERTY
COME TO THOSE WHO
ARE NOT DISCIPLINED.

- Book of Proverbs -

KEEP TURNING

The Jack-in-the-box -
A kid's toy?
Let's take a look.
The child turns the handle
until finally the goal is reached.
The toy clown pops out.
But what if the child
had stopped turning before the
box opened, before the clown
jumped out?
Sounds silly?
Of course it does.
Why stop before the success
is achieved.
The Jack-in-the-box.
Not just a kid's toy.
because it symbolizes what
can happen to us if we let
obstacles in our lives stop us
from pursuing our dreams.
In our lives, we stop turning

the handle before the dream pops out.
We give up on our goals when
success is just a turn away; when
success is just around the corner.
We become Jack's-in-the-box that
never have the chance to feel the
exhilaration of popping out - because
we give up on our dreams.
One more crank of the handle
and success could have been achieved.
But instead, we often let our temporary
setbacks force us to stop striving,
to stop turning the handle.
The Jack-in-the-box.
Just a kid's toy?
I don't think so.
The child never stops turning
until the clown pops out.
So, you should not stop until
your dream is reached...until
your goal is attained.
Just keep turning.

Many of life's failures are people who did not realize how close they were to success when they gave up.

- Thomas Edison -

Whatever the struggle
continue the climb
it may be only
one step to the summit.

- Diane Westlake -

Most people give up just when
they're about to achieve success,
they give up at the last
minute of the game, one foot
from a winning touchdown.

- H. Ross Perot -

Genius is only the power of making continuous efforts. The line between failure and success is so fine that we scarcely know when we pass it: so fine that we are often on the line and do not know it. How many a man has thrown up his hands at a time when a little more effort, a little more patience, would have achieved success. As the tide goes clear out, so it comes clear in. In business, sometimes, prospects may seem darkest when really they are on the turn. A little more persistence, a little more effort, and what seemed hopeless failure may turn to glorious success.

- Elbert Hubbard -

DON'T GIVE UP ON YOUR DREAMS

Can you see yourself in the White House?
Or in Yankee Stadium at home plate?
Can you picture yourself on an island,
Hand in hand with your soul mate?

Can you see yourself as a surgeon?
Or the head coach at the Final Four?
Possibly kicking the winning field goal,
To untie the Superbowl score?

Can you envision yourself as the anchor,
Of the nightly national news?
In front of the class as a teacher,
Sharing all your views?

How about an opera singer?
Or getting your Ph.D.?
Maybe running the Boston Marathon?
Or raising a family of three?

It doesn't matter what they are.
You must follow your dreams to the end.
Don't give up - be persistent!
Because one day you will win.

To give up on your dreams,
Like a bird without a voice -
You'd no longer have a purpose;
You'd no longer have a choice.

A choice to be what you want to;
To reach the pinnacle of success.
Once you give up on your dreams,
You can no longer achieve your best.

Some might say it cannot be done;
Others will laugh out loud.
Just remember there're only a few at the top,
On the bottom, there's a crowd.

Even your mind might try to convince you,
That your goal is way too tall.
But your will can overcome it,
So get back up when you fall.

They said it could never be done,
But Bannister ran the four-minute mile.
And soon after he did it,
Others completed this trial.

Just shows you anything can be done.
It's not as hard as it seems.
As long as you're willing to sacrifice,
And not give up on your dreams.

**Nothing can happen if it's not first a dream.
If you have someone with a dream, if you have
a motivated person with a goal and a vision, if you
have someone who never gives up, who has great
hope,
anything can happen.** — Jim Valvano -

Nothing in the world can take the place of persistence. Talent will not; nothing is more common than unsuccessful men with talent. Genius will not; unrewarded genius is almost a proverb. Education will not; the world is full of educated derelicts. Persistence and determination are omnipotent.
- Calvin Coolidge -

Hold fast to dreams
for if dreams die,
life is a broken
winged bird that
cannot fly.

- Langston Hughes -

The most serious crime
that man can commit
is the fraudulent act of
cheating himself,
of settling for less than
he deserves, of
remaining
at a level far below his
potential, of accepting
mediocrity,
when excellence is
within his reach....

- Christopher P. Neck -

↑

GOING UP?

Do you feel like giving up?
Possibly - giving in?
Because no matter how hard you try,
You never seem to win.

You exert a lot of effort;
Persevere when things get tough.
But despite all your dedication,
It's always just not enough.

Then consider these little parables;
See if you can relate.
Maybe they'll help clear your vision.
They might impact your fate.

Consider the determined athlete.
To win the gold was his quest.
But when the dust finally settled,
He ended up second best.

Or how about the young, aspiring lawyer,
In court, his very first day.
Although he had put in the hours,
The verdict failed to go his way.

And finally, the older woman,
Attempting to finish that degree.
Although she tried for the best marks,
On the paper appeared a "C."

But these stories are not over;
In fact, they've just begun.
These people lost the battle,
But the war - they eventually won.

You see, they <u>never</u> gave up,
Refused to quit or stop;
Through determination and desire,
They made it to the top.

The woman graduated with honors;
The man never lost another case;
The athlete broke a world record,
In a future race.

The lesson in all these stories;
Is that dreams don't come easily.
But don't ever stop pursuing,
Because one day they will be.

So as you strive to be the best,
It might help in always knowing,
It's not where you are that's important,
But in the direction you are going.

It's not so much where we are
that's important but in which direction
we are moving.

- Oliver Wendall Holmes -

The rewards for those
who persevere far exceed
the pain that must
precede the victory.

- Ted Engstrom -

Adversity causes some
men to break; others to
break records.

- W.A. Ward -

Success is to be measured not so much by the position
that one has reached in life, as by obstacles which he has
overcome while trying to succeed.
- Booker T. Washington -

To appreciate heaven well,
tis good for a man
to have some fifteen
minutes of hell.

- Will Carleton -

●

BEFORE THE RAINBOW

Have you ever felt so low,
Like rock-bottom was your home?
Your self-esteem had plummeted.
You felt so all alone.

One crisis after another.
Why me? you wanted to shout.
Depression clouded your outlook;
There seemed like no way out.

Then consider this quaint example.
Store it in your mind.
Recall it when necessary,
When happiness is hard to find.

An explorer stumbled across a diamond.
It seemed mediocre to him.
It appeared almost worthless;
Its sparkle, a faint dim.

Then he took a knife and file,
And cut it for some time.
And after many hours,
It suddenly began to shine.

The message in this story,
I hope rings loud and true -
That only through tribulations,
Can emerge the true you.

Difficulties are a part of life;
It's tough to overcome them.
But if you bear down and persevere,
You'll emerge as a brilliant gem.

So as you go through life,
Please remember to recall,
That before the rainbow appears,
There's usually some rainfall.

Like the diamond that is cut,
You'll be one of a kind.
By overcoming obstacles,
The more you will shine.

❀

Comfort and prosperity have never enriched the world as much as adversity has. Out of pain and problems have come the sweetest songs, and the most gripping stories. When we take chair lifts high in the Alps to see the scenery, we gaze down from dizzying heights and see some of the most beautiful flowers found anywhere. It's hard to believe that just a few weeks before, these flowers were buried under many feet of snow. The burdens of ice and winter storms have added to their luster and growth. Our burdens can have the same effect on our lives. As we face storms of adversity, we may rise with more beauty.

- Billy Graham -

The things which hurt, instruct.
- Benjamin Franklin -

There are no mistakes...the events
we bring upon ourselves, no matter
how unpleasant, are necessary in order
to learn what we need to learn; whatever
steps we take, they're necessary to reach
the places we've chosen to go.
- Richard Bach -

Difficult situations are
put in our way not
to stop us,
but to call out our courage
and our strengths.
- Unknown -

Happiness is not an absence of problems,
but the ability to deal with them.
- Unknown -

Sorrow makes us wise.
- Alfred, Lord Tennyson -

6

Who Am I?

Before you continue reading, please take a moment and complete this simple exercise. Take out a pencil and a sheet of paper. Now attempt to draw the keypad of your telephone without actually going and looking at the phone pad. Try to diagram from your memory the numbers, symbols, letters, etc. on the phone key pad. You have about two minutes to do this.

Finished? Now, compare your drawing with an actual phone keypad. Is your drawing a perfect representation of the keypad? If you are like many people, the drawing is not completely accurate. What does this mean? Well, this exercise should reveal that we do not really know and understand some of the things that we see and use everyday (e.g., the telephone), even though we might think we know these items. In the same way, there is something we see everyday, much more important than the phone, that we might think we know and understand but really do not. This something is ourself. Do you really know who you are and what your life's purpose is? Have you ever really sat down and examined your life and where it is headed? What are your needs, goals, desires, beliefs, values, your mission? Socrates once said, "The unexamined life is not worth living." Unless you examine who you are, you will wander aimlessly through your life, confused and frustrated. However, if you take the time for some self-examination, this will help you discover a purpose to follow and a direction to pursue. So look deeply into your soul to see who you are - not who others think you are. Ask yourself and then seek to answer a most important question: "Who am I?"

THE PATH TO UNIQUENESS

This is a simple ode
Of success - so to speak.
It's a moral of paving your own route,
Of how to be truly unique.

Consider the mediocre lad
Who wanted to stand out from the crowd.
He didn't want to be ordinary.
Conformity - he would not allow.

So he put on some bright new clothes,
Let his hair grow really long.
He thought now he was extra special.
"Different" was the name of his song.

But as this young man aged a little
And failed to reach his peak,
It all of a sudden dawned on him,
He must have used the wrong technique.

What this ordinary man realized;
He had been taking himself for a ride.
Even though he had changed his hairstyle,
He was still mediocre inside.

His realization was quite profound
And one quite easy to grasp
That to truly be extraordinary
Requires more than a simple task.

In order to blaze your own trail
Means more than an easy fix.
A cosmetic change won't ever suffice,
A new car won't do the trick.

The key message of this story -
That to make yourself unique
Is to do something better than others
In whatever field you might seek.

So whether you're an actress or a parent,
To stand tall above the rest.
Excellence should be your goal.
The reward will be success.

A man leaves all kinds of footprints when he walks through life. Some you can see, like his children and his house. Others are invisible, like the prints he leaves across other people's lives, the help he gives them and what he has said--his jokes, gossip that has hurt others, encouragement. A man doesn't think about it, but everywhere he passes, he leaves some kind of mark. All these marks added together are what a man means."

- Margaret Lee Runbeck -

My mother said to me, "If you are a soldier, you will become a general. If you are a monk, you will become the Pope." Instead, I was a painter, and became Picasso.
- Pablo Picasso -

Astronomers speak of the infancy, youth, maturity, and old age of stars and galaxies, acknowledging similarities with the stages of our own lives. For us, each life transition involves deep physical and psychological changes; the differences between one phase and another constitutes a new form or way of being. A former self dies and is replaced without disturbing the organic continuum of life.

- Robert Lawlor -

A life of frustration is inevitable for any coach whose
main enjoyment is winning.
- Chuck Noll -

*If you go and chase after women, you'll never meet quality women.
You only find quality women if you excel in your own life.*
- Kris Osborn -

No path leads to happiness;
The path itself is happiness.
- Buddha -

If I try to be like him, who will be like me?
- Yiddish proverb -

On April 10, 1994, I wrote these words, which I keep on my desk:
"Never again will I do anything for anyone that I don't feel
directly from my heart. I will not attend a meeting, make a phone
call, write a letter, sponsor or participate in any activity in which
every fiber of my being does not resound YES. I will act with the
intent of being true to myself.
- Oprah Winfrey -

But we all sort of hang out in that safety of mediocrity,
because to define yourself is a scary thing.
- M. Night Shyamalan -

A man's health can be judged by which he takes two at a
time---pills or stairs.
- Joan Welsh -

The most important thing in the Olympic games is not to win but to take part,
just as the most important thing in life is not the triumph but the struggle. The
essential thing is not to have conquered but to have fought well.
- Olympics motto by Baron Pierre de Coubertin -

I would rather be a superb meteor, every atom of me in
magnificent glow, than a sleepy and permanent
planet......
- Jack London -

If you are called to be a street sweeper,
sweep streets even as Michelangelo
painted, or Beethoven composed music, or
Shakespeare wrote poetry. Sweep streets
so well that all the hosts of heaven and
earth will pause to say, here lived a great
street sweeper who did his job well.
- Martin Luther King, Jr. -

Most gulls don't bother to learn more than the simplest fact of flight — how to get from shore to food and back again. For most gulls, it is not flying that matters but eating. For this gull, though, it was not eating that mattered, but flight. More than anything else, Jonathan Livingston Seagull loved to fly...the most

important thing in living was to reach out and touch

perfection in that which he most loved to do, and that was to fly.

- Richard Bach -
Jonathan Livingston Seagull

If you don't do it excellently, don't do it at all. Because if it's not excellent, it won't be profitable or fun, and if you're not in business for fun or profit, what the hell are you doing there?
- Robert Townsend -

139

Unless you go all out for something, you may conclude your life without actually having lived it. It doesn't have to be running, but it should be a quest for excellence, and it needs be for only that period of your life that it takes to fully explore it. That's how you find out what you are made of. That's how you find out who you are. To live your life your way, to reach for the goals you have set for yourself, to be the you that you want to be, that is success.

- Ron Dawes -
Olympic Marathoner

All successful employers are stalking men
who will do the unusual, men who
think, men who attract attention by performing
more than is expected of them.
- Charles M. Schwab -

Once you dedicate your life towards striving for excellence, you may not be in a class by yourself...but it won't take much time to call the roll.
- C. P. Neck -

Whatever is worth doing is worth doing well.
- Lord Chesterfield -

❖

FOOTPRINTS ON THE MIND

As we walk along the beach of life, we leave our footprints on the sand of all the people with whom we come in contact. Sometimes the crashing waves of people's thoughts wash away the footprints that we have left; and we are quickly forgotten. Other times, however, the impressions that we leave on others remain; the impression is not washed away by the tides of their minds. Why is it that some people's presence leaves lasting footprints on the shores of others' hearts; while others' contact quickly becomes a faded memory? The secret to leaving an impenetrable smile on the souls of others is not a function of the length of time spent with them. Does it really matter how long you keep your foot in the sand? Once the powerful crest reaches the shore, doesn't the footprint wash away no matter if your foot was in the sand for one hour or one minute? The answer lies not in the time spent with others but rather in the intensity of yourself as you cross that someone's path. You must completely give of your total self as you make contact with others. Treat this person as if you knew that they were going to die tomorrow. Intensify all of your energy in the moment. Do not worry about tomorrow or yesterday.

Your intensity will burn a lasting impression on those with whom you come in contact. As the child holds the magnifying glass to the leaf, what happens? The glass intensifies the light to burn an opening into the leaf. In the same way, your mind can become the magnifying glass that intensifies your thoughts and actions in order to penetrate the shell of those with whom you're in contact. Don't worry about the thoughts of others; this will make you hold back. Your footprint will then be easily swept away by the thunderous impact of the waves of their cognitions. Be intense, totally give of yourself, and your touch will be everlasting. Your footprints will remain on the beaches of all the people with whom you have come in contact during your life. Give it a try. The worst that can happen is that your footprint gets washed away. Better to have left a footprint that is washed away than not to have ever left a footprint at all.

Education does not exist to provide you with a job. Education is
here to nourish your soul.

- Ruth Simmons, Ph.D. -

Happiness comes only when we push
our brains and hearts to the farthest reaches
of which we are capable.
- Leo Rosten -

Death is not the greatest loss in life.
The greatest loss is what dies inside us while we live.
- Norman Cousins -

Perform every
act in life
as though it
were your last.

- Marcus Aurelius -

143

To live each day as though one's last,
never flustered, never apathetic, never attitudinizing -
here is the perfection of character.
- Marcus Aurelius -

There
      are
           no
              ordinary
                  moments.
- Dan Millman -

There is not a sprig of grass
that shoots uninteresting to me.
- Thomas Jefferson -

<u>Today</u> isn't any other day, you know.
- Lewis Carroll -

To burn always with this hard, gemlike flame,
to maintain this ecstasy, is success in life.
- Walter Pater -

♥

THE PLACE TO BEGIN...IS THE HEART

Sometimes when you're feeling kind of empty,
You're not feeling very rich,
You're not completely happy,
You feel it's time to make a switch.

Fulfillment is nowhere to be found.
Success is not within your range.
Then it's time to become who you really are;
It's time to make a change.

If you don't have any idea where to start,
You don't even have a clue,
Then follow this simple example
And see what it does for you.

There was a young man who owned a store.
The front was enclosed with glass
And twice a day, he'd wash this window
For the benefit of those who might pass.

Then one day he stood outside
And scrubbed till he could go no more.
As hard as he tried, it would not go away,
That one spot on the door.

After hours and hours, he finally gave up
And as he fell to his knees and cried,
An old man approached with the following advice.
He said, "Sir, the spot is inside."

The lesson should be crystal clear.
If you want to change what you are,
A new relationship will never suffice;
Not even a brand new car.

So don't settle for that status quo;
And if you're willing to pay the price,
Success and happiness is within your reach
If you follow this simple advice.

In order to become what you're capable of,
A few alterations might be the start,
But an outside change will do you no good;
The place to begin is the heart.

♥

It is not easy to find happiness in ourselves, and it is not possible to find it elsewhere.
- Agnes Repplier -

It is only with the heart that one can see rightly; what is essential is invisible to the eye.
- Antoine de St. Exupery -

The best and most beautiful things in the world
cannot be seen or even touched.
They must be felt with the heart.
- Helen Keller -

What lies behind us and what lies before
us are tiny matters compared to what lies within us.
- Ralph Waldo Emerson -

Happiness cannot come from without. It
must come from within. It is not what
we see and touch or that which others do
for us which makes us happy; it is that
which we think and feel and do, first for
the other fellow and then for ourselves.
- Helen Keller -

As long as anyone believes that his ideal and purpose is outside
himself, that it is above the clouds, in the past or in the future, he
will go outside himself and seek fulfillment where it cannot be
found. He will look for solutions and answers at every point
except the one where they can be found - in himself.
- Erich Fromm -

148

THE OCEAN OF LIFE

There is a magnificent ship sailing in the bright blue ocean. This vessel is filled to capacity with passengers. A storm all of a sudden develops. The ship is headed straight towards a pile of dangerous rocks. The captain, however, feels that the boat will somehow miss these threatening boulders. So instead of trying to alter the course of the boat, the captain instructs the first mate to start a party and to play music. The captain orders these instructions for the purpose of distracting the passengers so they don't focus upon the hazard that lies in their path. The party begins. The passengers are singing and laughing, having a grand old time. Then, without anyone realizing the danger ahead the boat thrashes onto the rocks. It capsizes.

In the ocean of life, we are the captains of our own ships. We tend to ignore the storms and the rocks that plague our lives. We fail to take the time to examine who we are and how we can really use our God-given talents to make this world a better place. Instead, we fill our lives with distractions such as parties, drugs, alcohol, jobs we don't enjoy, sexual encounters, in order to take our attention away from the rocks...to take our focus from the difficult questions that we need to ask ourselves. Questions like, "Who am I?" and "What is my purpose in life?" So, instead of disciplining ourselves and taking chances, we follow the well traveled route rather than changing the secure direction that our lives might be taking. Even though deep down inside we know something is wrong, we ignore this feeling and take a gamble that our ship will not hit the rocks...that our lives will be filled with contentment and happiness. But what happens? One day a sudden jolt wakes us up. We are startled to find that our lives have hit the rocks. We are depressed, lonely, and wonder how our lives took this course.

Remember, you are the captain of your life. Don't be fooled by the distractions. Have enough self-discipline to avoid them. Examine your life. If it is headed for the rocks, change your direction. You have the power to avoid the crash. Altering the course of your life will not be easy. It requires a tremendous amount of courage and strength to steer your life toward your dreams. The process will be filled with difficult obstacles...other rocks and other storms. However, the benefits far exceed these risks. The reward will be smooth sailing....

O

I am the master of my fate;
I am the captain of my soul.
- William Ernest Henley -

Our future may be beyond our vision
but it is not beyond our control.
- Robert Kennedy -

Ultimately, no one else has the answers to your unique set of
circumstances. You know best and are the one who must
take the necessary steps toward self-improvement.
- Alexandra Stoddard -

The unexamined life is not worth living.
- Socrates -

Not everything that is faced can be changed
but nothing can be changed until it is faced.
- James Baldwin -

There is only one corner of the universe you can be certain
of improving and that's your own self.
- Aldous Huxley -

THE COMPETITION IS WITHIN

You line up at the starting line
Or sit at your desk in class.
Thoughts might enter your head
About finishing first or last.

Consider the day of a salesman
Who sold double what he'd ever had.
But since some others sold three times as much,
He walked home feeling sad.

Or how about the marathon runner
Who completed the 26 miles.
But because she didn't win,
A grin - she would not allow.

When you compare yourself with your friends
To measure your success,
Winning is a function of others;
A comparison determines your best.

Instead, what I propose to you,
This measure is not up to par.
I suggest a different yardstick,
A better test of who you are.

Success is not the result
Of whether you lose or win.
The measure of achievement
Is how you feel within.

The goal should not be to better others
But to be the best you can be.
By overcoming your own limitations,
You'll discover victory.

The lesson should now be crystal clear;
To succeed again and again,
The contest is not against all the others,
The competition is within.

The virtue of all achievement is victory over oneself.
Those who know this victory can never know defeat.
                                                    - A. J. Cronin -

There is only one success - to be able to spend your life in your own way.
- Christopher Morley -

I cannot give you the formula for success,
but I can give you the formula for failure -
which is: try to please everybody.
- Herbert Bayard Swope -

When you are content to be simply yourself
and don't compare or compete, everybody will respect you.

- Lao-Tzu -

It is not the critic who counts; not the man who points out how the strong man stumbled, or where the doer of deeds could have done better. The credit belongs to the man who is actually in the arena; whose face is marred by dust and sweat and blood; who strives valiantly; who errs and comes short again and again; who knows the great enthusiasms, the great devotions, and spends himself in a worthy cause; who at the best knows in the end the triumph of high achievement; and who at the worst, if he fails, at least fails while daring greatly; so that his place shall never be with those cold and timid souls who know neither victory nor defeat.
- Theodore Roosevelt -

Hold yourself responsible for a higher standard than anybody else expects of you. Never excuse yourself.
- Henry Ward Beecher -

I have done my best. That is about all the philosophy of living that one needs.

- Lin Yutang -

THE RIGHT PATH

A young boy is riding in an airplane for the first time. He is amazed with curiosity, and he asks his mother if he can sit by the window so he can look at the towering sights below. Suddenly, the young lad notices an enormous mountain range beneath him. After a few minutes of gazing out the plane's window, he finally locates the highest point of this conglomeration of mountains; he is fixated upon the summit. As his glance becomes even more focused, he is suddenly intrigued by a unique sight. He leans over to his mom and shares with her the view before his eyes. He tells her he sees that there are many different paths leading to the top of the mountain. Some of the routes are direct - that is, they go straight from the valley below all the way to the summit. However, other paths curve and wind and curve again. Although these paths are less direct and less efficient, they eventually also reach the top of the mountain. After hearing these words from her son, his mother smiles lovingly at him. She gently touches the boy's arm and tells him that she is very impressed by his observation. She tells her son that there is a very powerful lesson to be learned from the observation that he just discovered. The son's curiosity is peaked once again, and he excitedly asks his mom to explain. While her son's eyes are transfixed on hers, the mother shares her story....

"You see son, you observed that there was not just one path that reached the mountain's highest point but rather there were many paths that led to the top of the mountain. Some routes were straight while others curved and meandered; yet, most of them eventually reached the top. Well son, in the same way, our life's journey is quite similar. In other words, the journey to success is like traveling to the top of the mountain. There are many different routes that lead to success - that lead to the top. Some people follow the trail of earning many educational degrees, others rear a family, some follow the path of starting their own business, while others try a combination of routes. Some people find the path that goes straight to the top really quickly, while others take many years to reach the pinnacle." The mother paused for a second; her son impatiently asked her to continue. "Son," she said, "you must realize that there is no one correct path to success. Each person must find the trail that is made for him or her. If you try to take a trail that is not made for you, you will never be able to attain the view from the top. If you try to be someone you really are not, your life will be one of misery and discontent; you'll never bathe in the calm waters of success. As Henry David Thoreau once said, 'If a man does not keep pace with his companions, perhaps it is because he hears a different drummer. Let him keep step to the music which he hears, however measured or far away.' Son, in the same way, you must step to music you hear; you must travel the path to success that is right for you. If you follow someone else's trail, you'll drop out halfway up the mountain before you ever taste the sweetness of success. Remember the effort you exert in your life toward finding your correct path to success will be well worth it. Your rewards will be inner peace and happiness - your reward will be success...your reward will be knowing who you really are...."

➤

If a man does not keep pace with his companions, perhaps it is because he hears a different drummer. Let him step to the music which he hears, however measured or far away.
- Henry David Thoreau -

Life is like a motion picture and everyone has their <u>own</u> part to play...So play that part to your best.
- Todd Denen -

The privilege of a lifetime is being who you are.
- Joseph Campbell -

Find a job you love, and you will never have to work another day in your life.
- Confucius -

Trust in what you love,
continue to do it,
and it will take you
where you need to go.
- Natalie Goldberg -

Do not follow where the path may lead.
Go instead where there is no path and leave a trail.

- Unknown -

There is at bottom only one problem
in the world and this is its name:
How does one break through?
How does one get into the open?
How does one burst the cocoon
and become a butterfly?
- Thomas Mann -

BE YOURSELF

Sometimes when you think you're on top of the world,
Everyone thinks you're an incredible guy.
You've done a good job of fooling the rest,
But you can't look yourself in the eye.

You've been living your life as others see fit,
Not listening to your voice inside;
You thought you were fooling everyone all along,
But you've been taking yourself for a ride.

If these words somehow hit you, straight in the heart
Like they were meant for you,
Perform this quaint example
And see what it makes you do.

Take a beach ball and fill it with air;
Fill it up till it's completely round.
Try and submerge it in a pool of water
And see what you have found.

You can lie on it, sit on it - do whatever you want;
You don't ever have to stop.
But soon you'll find, no matter what you try,
Eventually, it comes to the top.

It might only take a few minutes,
A few days, if you really care;
But time is no match for this inflatable toy.
Soon - it will reach the air.

The moral of this simple example
Is to dig down deep inside.
Find out who you really are
And then don't try to hide.

You can fool the whole world and even yourself
But this conceit will be only brief.
Your true self will surface and then rebel.
Your gain - will be only grief.

It's not too late to turn things around;
Start a new life, if you dare.
You'll be feeling content as you strive for the top
Like the beach ball rising for air.

In the long run it makes little difference how cleverly others are deceived; if we are not doing what we are best equipped to do, or doing well what we have undertaken as our personal contribution to the world's work, at least by way of an earnestly followed avocation, there will be a core of unhappiness in our lives which will be more and more difficult to ignore as the years pass.
- Dorothea Brande -

A musician must make music, an artist must paint, a poet must write, if he is to be at peace with himself. What a man must be, he must be.
- Abraham Maslow -

I may not be the fastest
I may not be the tallest
Or the strongest may not be the best
Or the brightest
But one thing I can do better
Than anyone else...
That is
To be me
- Leonard Nimoy -

**Do not wish to be anything
but what you are,
and try to be that perfectly.**
- St. Francis De Sales -

Your only obligation in any lifetime is to be true to yourself.
- Richard Bach -

Where your talents and the world's needs cross, there lies your vocation.

- Aristotle -

I was not born to be forced. I will breathe after my own fashion...
If a plant cannot live according to its nature, it dies; and so a man.

- Henry David Thoreau -

⚑

STAND UP FOR WHAT YOU BELIEVE

This is a little story
That should help you achieve.
It's about committing to your values;
It's about standing up for what you believe.

There was a young man who decided to try
To beautify his yard.
He decided he would do this task,
No matter how easy - or hard.

So he took a tree of five years
And put it in the ground.
But since he didn't plant it firmly,
This is what he found.

Whenever a strong wind came up
Or someone leaned against its branch,
This tree would abruptly turn over;
It would always lose its stance.

The lesson of this little example,
You are the sum of your beliefs,
So if you don't establish a position,
You will attain only grief.

So if you want to persevere
Through whatever life might bring,
Unless you commit to your values,
You'll fall for anything.

⚑

The purpose of life is to matter - to count,
to stand for something, to have it make some difference
that we lived at all....
- Leo Rosten -

He who has a <u>why</u> to live can bear with almost any <u>how</u>.
- Nietzsche -

If a man hasn't discovered
something that he will die for,
he isn't fit to live.
- Martin Luther King, Jr. -

The ultimate measure of a man is not where he stands in moments of comfort and convenience, but where he stands at times of challenge and controversy.
- Martin Luther King, Jr. -

Do you think they would believe us if we told them today what we know to be true? That after the pride of obtaining a degree and, maybe later, another degree and after their first few love affairs, that after earning their first big title, their first shining new car and traveling around the world for the first time and have had it all...they will discover that none of it counts unless they have something real and permanent to believe in.
- Mario Cuomo -

The wise and moral man shines like a fire on a hilltop.
- The Pal. Canon -

THE JOURNEY

A young woman searches for happiness
In addition to searching for truth.
She tries to discover true peace
During the early days of her youth.

She climbs the highest mountains,
She covers uncharted ground,
Expending much of her energy
In hopes that the answer will be found.

After all the stones are turned over
And the searcher has slowed her stride,
The older woman finally realizes
That the answer was always inside.

The meaning to life is not in a book
Or on the ocean floor.
It's not at the end of a rainbow
Or waiting behind some hidden door.

True peace is inside each of us,
In every boy and girl,
Measured not by money or education
But in how we view the world.

We must truly love ourselves
And greet others with a smile.
Live each day to the fullest
Instead of saying, "Someday, I'll."

If we stumble along the way
Or the results don't pass the test,
We should walk with pride and dignity
If we know we did our best.

As we live each day to the fullest,
We must not forget to recall,
"It is better to have tried and failed
Than not to have tried at all."

Now that her search is almost over,
The answer is a revelation,
The significance is the JOURNEY
And not the destination.

Throw away all ambition
beyond that of doing the day's work well.
The travelers on the road to success live
in the present, heedless
of taking thought for the morrow.
Live neither in the past nor in the future,
but let each day's work absorb your entire energies,
and satisfy your wildest ambition.

- William Osler -

My success has been the harvest of what happens when you love the "thing"
more than the results; in my case, the thing is comedy - that is my primary
relationship in life.

- Jerry Seinfeld -

Paradise is where I am.

- Voltaire -

You can always find the sun within yourself if you will
only search.
- Maxwell Maltz -

When one is a stranger to oneself,
then, one is estranged from others, too.
- Anne Morrow Lindbergh -

INNER PEACE PARADOX

The word *paradox* is derived from the Latin root "paradoxes," which means "conflicting with expectation." An example of a "conflict with expectation" involves the search for inner peace. Let me explain.

Picture in your mind a large circle. Within this circle is another circle. Within this circle is another circle...and on and on and on and on until in the center of this picture is the smallest circle possible surrounded by an infinite number of circles. "What does this picture represent," you might ask. This exhibit represents the "inner peace paradox." More specifically, as we travel through the soul-searching process toward inner peace, a paradox occurs.

Each circle in the picture represents a separate step along our journey toward inner peace. As we travel from a smaller circle to a larger circle, this signifies progression toward finding out who we really are. The smallest circle in the picture represents the very first stage in the inner peace journey. It represents that point where we first become aware of those nagging questions deep within our souls. Questions such as, "Who am I?" or "What am I supposed to do with my life?" In order to progress to the next circle, to the next step toward inner peace, we must attempt to answer those initial questions. However, by attempting to answer these initial questions, this generates more questions. This is the inner peace paradox. One might think that as one travels along his/her path toward inner peace, the questions will become fewer. This is a myth. The paradox occurs in that in actuality, as one begins to know himself more completely, the greater the number of questions generated. In other words, as one begins to learn about oneself, the more one realizes how much there really is to know. Thus, the inner peace journey is depicted from going from the smaller circle to the largest one rather than from the largest one to the smallest, as one might initially expect.

However, it is important to note that even though more questions are being generated as each step is accomplished, this is progression because as each circle becomes larger (each new step is reached), the more one becomes aware of who one really is.

Should the journey be taken alone or with someone? It depends. If the journey is taken by someone who has determined on their own that they truly do want to take the journey and who is on a similar pace as you, then this will allow you to proceed more quickly on the journey than if you went solo. This is because you will have someone to help answer those questions. However, if you attempt to bring a partner on this exploration who does not really want to go along...beware. This will slow your progress immensely - like two people rowing a boat where one is out of sync. The boat goes in circles. In the same way, if your partner is out of sync with you, you will just go in circles during your inner peace journey. Thus, no progress will be made and you will experience much anxiety and frustration.

Remember, you are responsible for your progression in this journey. NEVER let anyone or anything interfere with your travels toward excellence. Life is too precious.

...I'm doing what I should have done years ago,
which is finding out who I am and what I want.
I want to have a choice. And when I made decisions through choice, not duty, it has to be better for me and for the people who love me and the people I love.
- Louise Fletcher -

We must be trying to learn
who we really are rather
than trying to tell ourselves
who we should be.
- John Powell -

We must not cease from exploration and the end
of all our exploring will be to arrive where we began
and to know the place for the first time.
- T. S. Eliot -

All men should strive
to learn before they die
what they are running from,
and to, and why.

- James Thurber -

The important thing is not to stop questioning.
One cannot help but be in awe when he
contemplates the mysteries of eternity, of life, of
the marvelous structure of reality. It is enough if
one tries merely to comprehend a little of this
mystery every day.
- Albert Einstein -

7

Helping Others

Margaret Runbeck wrote:

> A man leaves all kinds of footprints when
> he walks through life. Some you can see like
> his children and his house. Others are invisible
> like the prints he leaves across other people's
> lives, the help he gives them and what he has
> said - his jokes, gossip that has hurt others,
> encouragement. A man doesn't think about it,
> but everywhere he passes, he leaves some kind
> of mark. All these marks added together are
> what a man means.

With these words in mind, a question to ponder is, "What type of footprints are you leaving on your beach of life?" As you climb the ladder to success, do you have one hand free to help others up a few steps or are you oblivious to others' needs? Truly successful individuals have remarked that one of their secrets to success is that they always tried to help other people overcome their personal obstacles. What these successful individuals discovered is what some philosophers have been trying to tell us for centuries...that is, by helping others, we help ourselves in return. By helping others, you will feel a sense of worth and well-being that will energize your efforts toward achieving your own goals. In other words, the more positive "footprints" you make during your life, the more successful you will be.

✈

GIVING WINGS

This is a simple story
Of helping others to achieve their dreams.
It's about love and friendship;
It's not as hard as it seems.

A man was walking along the seashore,
And as he paced the sandy ground,
He stumbled upon a creature -
A bird is what he found.

He brought it home and thought that
Putting it in a cage was the thing.
But after just a little while,
The bird forgot how to sing.

The message of this story,
Whether it's your mate or your child -
If you don't let them spread their wings,
They'll lose the urge to smile.

By helping someone reach their goals,
There is no greater gift.
An impenetrable bond is created,
Giving both of you a lift.

So remember the ones you love.
And please help them to try
To be the best they're capable of
By allowing them to fly.

✈

They may forget what you said, but they will never forget how you made them feel..
- Carl W. Buechner -

LOVE DOESN'T SIT THERE, LIKE A STONE. IT HAS TO BE MADE, LIKE BREAD; RE-MADE ALL THE TIME, MADE NEW.
- Ursula K. LeGuin -

The mediocre teacher tells.
    The good teacher explains.
        The superior teaching demonstrates.
           The great teacher inspires.
                - William A. Ward -

Everyone has the power for greatness----not for fame but greatness, because greatness is determined by service.
- Martin Luther King, Jr. -

The only certain means of success is to render more and better service than is expected of you, no matter what your task may be.
- Og Mandino -

**Be kind, for everyone you meet
is fighting a great battle.**
- Philo of Alexandria -

*Outstanding leaders go out of the way to boost
the self-esteem of their personnel. If people believe
in themselves, it's amazing what they can accomplish.*
- Sam Walton -

**Great leaders have one primary goal - that
is,
to help individuals to lead themselves.**
- Charles Manz -

Our chief want is someone who will inspire us to be what we know
we could be.
- Ralph Waldo Emerson -

> The ultimate responsibility of a leader is to facilitate
> other people's development as well as his own.
> - Fred Pryor -

**Ideal teachers use themselves as bridges
over which they invite their students to cross;
then having facilitated their crossing, joyfully
collapse,
encouraging them to create bridges of their
own.**
- Nikos Kazantzakis -

A great teacher never strives to explain her vision;
she simply invites you to stand beside her and see for yourself.
- Rev. R. Inman -

BE GENTLE

Please be gentle
To the beggar on the street.
Be gentle...
To all those whom you meet.

Be kind...
To the old lady in your lane.
Be compassionate...
To the attendant on the plane.

Be gentle...
Because everyone in your path
Is fighting very hard,
Fighting to try and grasp

The meaning of their life
And the battles they must fight;
Some just trying to figure out
How to make it through the night.

So give unconditionally
From the very start
Because everyone, behind their mask,
Conceals a fragile heart.

We are all climbing our personal mountain,
One that's physical or mental.
So offer your hand to those in need,
And most of all...**Be gentle**....

> ## What do we live for if it is not to make life less difficult for each other.
> — George Eliot —

> Kindness is the oil that takes the friction out of life.
> - Anonymous -

> If thine enemy be hungry,
> give him bread to eat;
> and if he be thirsty,
> give him water to drink.
> - Proverbs 25:21 -

*The important thing in life is not stopping
to smell the roses...
but rather picking them for someone special.*

— Banks T. Adams III —

Success in life has nothing
to do with what you gain in
life or accomplish for yourself.
It's what you do for others.
- Danny Thomas -

**The miracle is this--
the more we share,
the more we have.**

- Leonard Nimoy -

The great mind knows the power of gentleness.
- Robert Browning -

☆

YOU CAN MAKE A DIFFERENCE

There is nothing I can do,
A lot of times we say
To make this world a better place;
To make problems go away.

People die of starvation
In poverty-stricken lands.
What difference can we make?
Why should I lend a hand?

What impact could I make?
This is what most will reply.
For every two I save,
There'll be several hundred that die.

The earth's problems are way too big;
It's no use in even trying
To help those that are needy;
To help those that might be crying.

But, no matter how large,
No matter how massive,
There is just no excuse
To turn our heads and be passive.

The answer that I propose to you
Is to alter your frame of view.
Don't look at problems globally,
But rather from what each of us can do.

What I'm trying to say right here -
We should all lend a helping hand
To make this world a better place;
It's time to take a stand.

Start by helping those around you.
A pleasant smile is a way to begin.
And soon it will become habit;
A beautiful cycle that never ends.

As you help someone during the day,
A smile is what you'll earn;
And tell the one you've touched
To help someone in return.

And soon, before your eyes,
Like falling dominoes, in a row,
You'll see people aiding others.
A helping seed - beginning to grow.

These once global problems
Might one day disappear
Because by looking at something differently,
It helps to reduce the fear -

The fear that problems are too large
To give a helping hand.
Now that this chain has already started,
It might spread across the land.

Start this very moment
Because now you know the solution.
We can make this world a better place
If we all make a contribution.

You can help to solve world peace
Or assist an elder across the street.
How about teaching someone to read
Or putting shoes on some child's feet.

Maybe volunteering at a hospital
Or sending money to the poor;
Helping your parents around the house;
Assisting someone through the door;

Refusing to use plastic bags;
Not throwing trash on the ground;
Letting someone get in front of you;
Picking someone up when they're down.

It doesn't matter what you do
Because soon, you will learn
That by giving yourself to others,
You'll help yourself in return.

The greatest use of life is to spend it for something that will outlast it.

- William James -

We are here to add what we can to life,
not to get what we can from it.
- William Osler -

My research offers impressive evidence
that we feel better when we attempt to make
our world better...
to have a purpose beyond one's self
lends to existence a meaning and direction--
the most important characteristic of high well-bring.

- Gail Sheehy -

There is but one unconditional commandment...
to bring about the very largest total universe
of good which we can see.
- William James -

Our goal is to <u>influence</u> history
instead of merely observing it.
- John F. Kennedy -

One generation plants the trees;
another sits in their shade.
- Chinese Proverb -

◆

THE MISSING PIECE?

The young man sees his life as a jigsaw puzzle
That he put together, so carefully.
Then one day he realizes one piece is missing;
He wonders where it could be.

He tried to force other pieces he finds
That really don't belong;
He tries to convince himself that they fit
But deep down he knows that he's wrong.

This one missing piece might be the job he wants
Or the soul mate he never knew.
It might be that car he's always dreamed of
Or that house near the ocean blue.

He continues to hunt for that one missing part,
Expending his energy along the path,
Thinking that once he finally finds it,
Happiness will be in his grasp.

After years of searching and trying to find it,
Not leaving any stones unturned,
He sits back and ponders the meaning of it all;
And this is what he eventually learned.

His life's puzzle was really always complete,
Even without that one missing piece
Because in reality, it was never gone;
It was always within his reach.

The piece was not a fancy house
Or the trip of his life;
It was certainly not winning the lottery
Or one day meeting his wife.

The missing piece was never gone,
But where could it be?
He had spent so much time searching outside
That he could never see

That he could have spent over one hundred years
Searching for this one missing part
Because it was nowhere outside to be found;
It was always inside his heart.

The piece was not a material object
Or something he could spend.
Rather, it was a lesson to one day learn;
To perform again and again.

He learned that by <u>giving</u> to others
Rather than focus on a receipt,
He truly helped himself
Make his puzzle complete.

◆

I shall pass through this world but once.
Any good therefore that I can do, or any kindness
that I can show to any human being, let me do it now.
Let me not defer nor neglect it, for I shall not pass this
way again.
- Victor Hugo -

**It is one of the most beautiful compensations
of this life that no man can sincerely try to help
another without helping himself.**
- Ralph Waldo Emerson -

*You cannot do a kindness too soon for you never
know how soon it will be too late.*
- Ralph Waldo Emerson -

> *A generous action is its own reward.*
> - William Walsh -

> The more he gives to others,
> the more he possesses of his own.
> - Lao-Tzu -

> You can't make yourself bigger by making other people smaller.
> - Herzberg -

> Those who bring sunshine to the lives
> of others cannot keep it from themselves.
> - Sir James Barrie -

> One word frees us of
> all the weight and pain
> in life: That word is love.
> - Sophocles -

HOLDING ON MEANS LETTING GO

There was a very young girl
Attempting to fly her kite.
And as the wind grew stronger and stronger,
The child held on with all her might.

But instead of letting more string out,
She thought holding on was all she could do,
And in only just a few seconds,
The kite string broke in two.

The kid was quite perplexed
As a tear ran down her face.
The kite was hers no longer
As it drifted into space.

As I hope this example illustrates,
You must consider this to be truth -
Gripping tighter might not be the answer;
Sometimes you have to let loose.

Whether it's a relationship or your child,
There is something you must know -
That in order to hold on,
Sometimes you have to let go.

The basic cause of most inharmonious human
relationships is the tendency to impose our values on
other people.
- Robert Anthony -

The only way in which one
human being can properly attempt
to influence another is by encouraging
him to think for himself, instead of
endeavoring
to instill ready-made opinions into his head.
- Leslie Stephen -

Consider how hard it is to change yourself and you'll understand what little chance you have of trying to change others.

- Jacob M. Braude -

LEARNING TO LIVE IS LEARNING TO LET GO.
- Sogyal Rinpoche -

✦

A PEBBLE OR A STONE?

There is a famous saying;
To the ears, it's quite a treat.
"I complained I had no shoes,
Till I saw a man without any feet."

In life we come across people
Who complain of having "no shoes."
But before you point a finger,
Please consider their point of view.

Ponder the middle-aged man,
Once possessing a full head of hair.
But one morning his reflection revealed
Many strands were no longer there.

Or how about the pretty young woman
Whose breasts were somewhat small.
But whenever she looked in the mirror,
She perceived none at all.

These problems to an outsider
Might seem trivial at best.
But to their individual owners,
They're obstacles to success.

What you might see as a grain of sand,
They might view as a stone.
What you envision as solitude,
They might see as "alone."

The message in these simple words,
I hope is clear to all.
What's a challenge to another,
To you might seem quite small.

So don't judge the problems of your friends;
Rather, support them in their quest
To overcome their obstacles,
As they strive to be their best.

✦

**Resolve to be Tender with the Young
Compassionate with the Aged
Sympathetic with the Striving
And Tolerant of the Weak and Wrong.**

**Sometime in life you will
have been all of these
yourself.**
- Unknown -

Compassion is a spirituality
as if creation mattered. It
is treating all creation
as holy and as divine...
which is what it is.
- Matthew Fox -

Friendship makes prosperity more shining
and lessens adversity by dividing and sharing it.
- Cicero -

Sorrow shared is halved
and joy shared is doubled.
- Native American Saying -

Epilogue

T.S. Eliot once wrote:

> We must not cease from exploration
> and the end of all our exploring
> will be to arrive where we began
> and to know the place for the first time.

I hope our exploration together through the pages of <u>Medicine for the Mind</u> has helped you to see yourself in a more unique and positive manner. I hope that in some way the material in these pages have served as a catalyst for you to begin and/or continue the difficult, yet wonderful process of pursuing your grandest dreams. In fact, I would value your feedback on how this book may have benefited you. Please email me at christopherneck@yahoo.com or write to me at the following address:

> Department of Management
> Virginia Tech
> Blacksburg, Virginia 24061

From the bottom of my heart and soul, I thank you for trusting me and taking this journey with me through the plethora of motivational and inspirational stories, poems, and quotes. By reading this book, you have already taken the first step toward making your fantasies a reality. Continue the adventure. You now have the mental tools to "build your own bridges" to your dreams. I know you will experience the sweet taste of success. I believe in you.

Life is Magical!

Christopher P. Neck

Index

Fromm, Erich, 148
Future, 56

G

Generosity, 196
Genius, 81
Gentleness, 185–86, 188
Gide, Andre, 48
Giving, 180–81, 193–94, 196
"Giving Wings", 180–81
Goals, 54–55, 56, 57, 82, 101, 115–16, 121, 140
Goddard, John, 19
Goethe, 24
"Going Up?", 123–24
Goizueta, Roberto, 96
Goldberg, Natalie, 160
Graham, Billy, 129
Gratitude, 34–35
Greatness, 106, 110, 182
Griffith, John L., 73
Growth, 49

H

"Handfuls of Gifts", 34–35
Hansen, Grace, 12
Happiness, 24, 130, 137, 143, 147, 148
Hardwork, 70–71
Hard work, 73, 74, 77, 78, 82, 83–84, 85–86, 87–88, 89
Harvey, Paul, 102
Hayden, Sterling, 49
Health, 72, 138
Heart, 145–46, 147
Help and Food, 78
Helping, 180–81, 188, 193–94, 195
Hemingway, Ernest, 12
Herzberg, 196
"Holding On Means Letting Go", 197
Holmes, Oliver Wendall, 125
Horace, 16, 20, 32
Hubbard, Elbert, 118

Hughes, Langston, 122
Hugo, Victor, 195
Hustle, 13–14, 15
Huxley, Aldous, 152
Huxley, T.H., 101

I

Idleness, 72
Impossibilities, 45
Impossible limitations, 36
Inaction, 15, 16, 19, 77
Influence, 192
Inman, R., 184
Inner peace, 172, 173–74
"Inner Peace Paradox", 173–74
Intelligence, 73, 98
Intensity, 141–42
Interest, 74
Iococca, Lee, 7

J

Jacks, L.P., 45
Jackson, Andrew, 19
James, William, 33, 191, 192
Jefferson, Thomas, 144
Johnson, Nikosi, 6
Johnson, Samuel, 106
"The Journey", 169–70
Joy, 203

K

Kaiser, Henry J., 44
Kazantakis, Nikos, 184
"Keep Turning", 115–16
Keller, Helen, 49, 147, 148
Kennedy, John F., 15, 192
Kettering, Charles, 56
Kindness, 180–81, 182, 183, 185–86, 187, 189–90, 195, 196, 202
King, Martin Luther Jr., 138, 167, 168, 182